POLICING SPACE

POLICING SPACE

Territoriality and the
Los Angeles Police Department

Steve Herbert

University of Minnesota Press
Minneapolis
London

Published by the University of Minnesota Press
111 Third Avenue South, Suite 290, Minneapolis, MN 55401-2520
Printed in the United States of America on acid-free paper
Third Printing, 2000

Library of Congress Cataloging-in-Publication Data

Herbert, Steven Kelly, 1959–
    Policing space : territoriality and the Los Angeles Police
Department / Steve Herbert.
        p.   cm.
    Includes bibliographical references and index.
    ISBN 0-8166-2864-5 (hardcover)
    ISBN 0-8166-2865-3 (pbk.)
    1. Los Angeles (Calif.) Police Dept.   2. Police — California — Los
Angeles.   3. Police power — California — Los Angeles.   4. Human
territoriality — California — Los Angeles.   I. Title.
HV8148.L55H47   1996
363.2'09794'94 — dc20   96-20333

CONTENTS

PREFACE AND ACKNOWLEDGMENTS

LIKE MILLIONS OF OTHERS, I was stunned by the video-tape of the beating administered to Rodney King by a group of Los Angeles Police Department officers in March 1991. The continuing flurry of blows, King's hopeless attempts to defend himself, and the impassivity of the many officers who were watching all seemed incommensurate with any pre-tense on the part of the LAPD to be a model police agency. It seemed inconceivable that such a massive and unnecessary use of force could be condoned by a large group of officers, that their efforts to control space might regularly rely upon bru-tality of this nature. Repeated viewings of the videotape have failed to reduce my horror at what it depicts.

As much as the videotape sickened me, it also compelled me with its questions. I wondered just how a social agency entrusted with the power to administer lethal force could overstretch its limits in such a profound and dramatic way.

Race immediately suggested itself as an important factor, but a full explanation was probably more complex. The question of why those officers chose to respond to King in that way demanded investigation.

The King beating occurred while I was surveying literature that draws connections between the exercise of power and the control of space. I found this literature instructive but was frustrated by its frequent lack of empirical substantiation. There were too few discussions of how actual agencies of power exercise their control over space, of exactly how territorial control underlies social control. An up-close look at the LAPD seemed an opportunity to measure these more abstract considerations against the practices of an important and politically charged social agency.

This book is the ultimate result of my effort to examine, in a detailed fashion, a particular agency that daily exercises its power by exercising control over space. As my analysis illustrates, the processes by which police officers socially construct and attempt to control the spaces they patrol lie at the heart of contemporary policing; indeed, as I show, satisfying each of the imperatives that impel police action requires the officers to control space. But the processes by which officers make and mark space are complex, and thus to explain the spatial exercise of police power is to throw the motivations of that power into particularly sharp relief. My investigation not only sees policing in a new way, but also reveals the complicated processes by which territorial control is manifested in daily practice.

That I entered the world of the LAPD at all was due largely to the efforts of Jack Greene, who kindly shepherded my request through the appropriate channels. Jack also helped by providing insights into the LAPD that were useful in my efforts to analyze what I witnessed. For giving final approval for the fieldwork, I thank Chief Willie Williams; his willingness to grant my request is but one symbol of the different LAPD he is attempting to construct.

I was assisted by several others within the LAPD, most of whom must remain anonymous. I *can* mention Dan Keonig, Gerry Mears, J. I. Davis, John Mutz, Margaret York, and Lymon Doster, all of whom helped open doors and answer questions. The other LAPD personnel who did so much to help me understand their world cannot be singled out, but I owe them a tremendous debt for discussing their work with me at a politically turbulent time. Much of what follows was made possible only by their generosity with their time and their willingness to answer my many questions.

In the world of academia, I was blessed with the assistance of numerous people in the construction and execution of this project. Allen Scott and Ed Soja encouraged me to improve the theoretical rigor of the work, while Bob Emerson worked to ensure a clear link between theory and data. Eric Monk-konen's enthusiastic support meant much through the writing and rewriting process. Nick Entrikin helped make the analysis cohesive and also provided important support at key moments. And Gerry Hale worked tirelessly to improve all aspects of the work.

Many others read all of the manuscript and provided suggestions or encouragement or both; they include Craig Holnick, Michael Hooper, Peter Manning, Gary Marx, Robert Sack, and two anonymous reviewers. Others — namely, Nick Blomley, Ben Forest, Nick Fyfe, Peter Jackson, Steve Mastrofski, and Ralph Saunders — read part of the manuscript and were similarly helpful. I know I have not satisfied all of them with my revisions, but the work is clearly better as a result of my efforts to attend to their suggestions.

Thanks also to everyone at the University of Minnesota Press — namely, Janaki Bakhle, Mary Byers, Lisa Freeman, Jeff Moen, and Carrie Mullen — whose efficiency, responsive-

ness, and competence have made the publication process pain-
less and actually enjoyable. Special thanks to Lynn Marasco
for excellent copyediting.

Two other people deserve special mention. Joe Nevins has
been a steadfast colleague and friend whose passion did more
to motivate me than he undoubtedly ever realized. And Kath-
erine Beckett has been an unswerving source of support, advice, critique, diversion, and love. The worth of her gifts to me
escapes estimation.

Finally, I would like to acknowledge the lifelong support
of my family, in particular my parents, Connie and Harvey,
and my sister, Anne.

INTRODUCTION

IT HAD BEEN A TYPICAL Saturday night in the Wilshire Division—the call load was high, the range of calls variable (from loud parties to shots fired), the need for help from units from other divisions occasional. It was typically busy, but not especially eventful.

This busy complacency was shattered by the sudden dominance on the radio by reports of a pursuit. The chase actually began in the Hollywood Division but took over the Wilshire frequency because the two units are contiguous. And, indeed, the pursuit flowed into Wilshire, where, near a busy intersection, the suspect stopped his newly stolen car and went "underground," police lingo for trying to hide. The sergeant decided to respond.

We arrived at an impressive scene. Above us circled an "air unit," a helicopter whose 30 million candlepower "night-sun" illuminated the one-square-block area that presumably contained the car thief. Four police cars, we were told, had formed a "perimeter"; that is, they were positioned on each of the four streets forming the block, the better to sight the fleeing suspect. In addition, several officers were milling about the "command post" set up in the parking lot of a closed gas station, all of them learning about their particular responsibilities. Four of them, for example, were to follow the two police dogs and their respective handlers, and thus be positioned to handcuff the suspect should the dogs detect him. A number of supervisory personnel were present as well: a sergeant from the Hollywood Division who had primary responsibility, another Hollywood sergeant serving as his aide, a sergeant from Wilshire (other than the one escorting me) there to observe the Wilshire officers involved. In addition, the captain who heads the Metro Division of the Los Angeles Police Department — the organizational home for such special units as SWAT (Special Weapons and Tactics), the Mounted Unit (the horses), and the K-9 unit — was also observing. (Although he was the highest-ranking officer there, he did not assume control of the scene; because a Hollywood officer began the pursuit, his sergeant was considered in charge.) And over us all orbited the helicopter, whose public address system was eventually used to communicate a loud message to the suspect that the dogs were about to come in, and that he should surrender.

Unfortunately, I was not able to witness the incident to its conclusion. Another thief struck in another part of the division, and the sergeant I was with, recognizing his redundancy at the command post, lurched off on his own potential pursuit. Nonetheless, the scene raises a number of provocative questions. Why were so many human and technical resources devoted to the capture of a simple car thief? Why the incredible array of sophisticated procedures? Why the immense investment of time? Why the neglect of the continuing pileup of calls in both the Hollywood and the Wilshire Divisions? What accounts for the variety of territorial practices developed to locate and corral an elusive suspect—the elaborate communications devices to follow the pursuit, the surveillance from the sky, the hopefully impermeable "perimeter" set up around the block that contained the suspect?

In the analysis that follows, I offer a wide-ranging answer to these questions; I develop an understanding of how and why police exercise territoriality, understood here, following Sack, as "a spatial strategy to affect, influence, or control resources and people, by controlling area."[1] I argue not only that such spatial strategies are fundamental to police power, but also that they are best understood as arising from the workings of six "normative orders" central to the structure of police organizations: law, which by legislative fiat defines the permissible parameters of police action; bureaucratic regulations, which seek to determine police procedures more finely through a set of rules that establish a chain of command; adventure/machismo, which constitutes the police as courageous individuals who embrace danger as a test of individual ability; safety, which establishes a set of practices to protect the police from undue harm; competence, which suggests that police should be able to control the public areas for which they are responsible; and morality, which infuses police practice with a sense of right and goodness, in essence because it helps protect society from the "bad guys."

Indeed, all of these normative orders structured the behavior in and around the gas station command post. The law defined police crime control responsibilities and dictated how and where officers could search; bureaucratic regulations defined who was to assume what responsibilities; a sense of adventurousness permeated all discussions of the chase and the ongoing attempt to corral the suspect; safety considerations helped explain the presence of both the helicopter and the dogs; a sense of competence demanded the seizure of not just any criminal, but one who had run from the police; and a sense of moral right accompanied the attempt to enable the owner of the car, brought to the scene by a Hollywood officer, to witness the bringing of the offender to justice.

What follows is an elaboration of these normative orders and an explanation of how each shapes the territorial practices of the police. I define normative order in a quite specific and idiosyncratic way, as a set of rules and practices centered on a primary value (see Table 1). This definition explicitly weds rules and values, and thus links actions with their motivations. It provides, in other words, a systematic way of understanding the primary mechanisms by which police behavior is both structured and given meaning. In addition, an analysis that investigates a variety of normative orders provides a means to explain conflict. Different normative orders may cohere, as in the incident described here, but they also frequently conflict. The normative orders of law and adventure/ machismo, for example, can cohere when a bold officer enforces the law aggressively. But they conflict when an officer, hell-bent on demonstrating courage, chooses to override various legal restrictions on access to private places or the use of force.

Table I. The normative orders of police territoriality

Order	Primary value(s) for officers
Law	Preserving legal regulations
Bureaucratic control	Maintaining internal order through chain of command and differentiation of responsibilities
Adventure/machismo	Demonstrating courage and strength
Safety	Preserving life
Competence	Demonstrating capability and worthiness of respect
Morality	Demonstrating goodness by triumphing over evil

It is impossible to state in advance precisely which order will have greater purchase on each officer. Different officers, in different ranks, and at different times and places, will disagree about which order is most significant. This explains the regular conflicts that erupt within the organization.

It may seem misguided, at first glance, to treat these six orders as functionally equivalent. The law, for instance, is constructed and debated in explicit and formalized ways and thus differs fundamentally from the less formal ethos of machismo. My analysis, however, shows that each order works in a similar fashion to structure the behavior of police officers who regularly seek to create order through controlling space. My focus is on the daily practices of officers and the processes by which they enact these orders through their geopolitical maneuvers. At this level, each order structures and provides meaning for the actions officers undertake.

Each order, then, contributes crucially to the ways that police officers conceptualize the areas they patrol and how they mobilize to control those areas, how they *make* and *mark* space. In what follows, I demonstrate the centrality of territorial action to everyday police behavior and explain that action comprehensively.

Given the long-standing and well-publicized claims that LAPD officers are prone to racist excesses, it may seem surprising that I do not include racism as one of my normative orders. But racist considerations are not regularly and overtly invoked in individual or collective decisions concerning how to define and control space; they are not often consciously and reflexively employed in territorial understandings and behavior. This does not mean that race is irrelevant to policing. Instead, it means that racial considerations shape which normative order(s) officers mobilize to interpret and enact a situation. For example, officers are more likely to see minority-dominated areas as unsafe and morally unclean, as places where they can find dangerous foes against which they can act with masculine aggressiveness. The result is a more confrontational and less nuanced policing that creates tension between residents and officers. In other words, racial understandings are not expressed overtly, but more subtly *through* the central normative orders that officers invoke to make and mark space.

Territorial action has been noted by other scholars of the police, but not analyzed fully or systematically.[2] This may be because such action is so commonplace as to seem unremarkable; most significant police actions involve some sort of enforcement via movement of people in space. This is most obvious in the power the police most frequently threaten and often carry out—the power to jail. But it is also crucial to managing interpersonal disputes and other mundane ongoing challenges the police face. It is crucial to keeping business owners free from the sight of homeless people bothering their customers, to keeping residents of a neighborhood free from the fear of clusters of young people on their lawns. Indeed, it is only with the capacity to control and clear space that the police are in many situations able to restore the order they are presumed to maintain.

Territorial control is an inherent outcome of the social organization of the police. As Silver points out, modern policing has meant the development of a capacity to intrude into and control space; policing is a power that can be "widely diffused throughout civil society in small and discretionary operations that are capable of rapid concentration."[3] I will be discussing many of these "small and discretionary operations" and illuminating their centrality to daily policing. But the general mandate to control certain spaces at certain times does not define exactly how and why territorial power will be mobilized. It is thus important to investigate the variety of motivations that structure police territorial practices.

A detailed explication of these motivations is only possible via an ethnographic study. Only through closely examining the daily practices of officers can one develop a nuanced and comprehensive understanding of police territoriality; it is in and through these practices that normative orders are enacted in space. But ethnography contains an implicit intellectual tradeoff that favors intensive analysis over extensive comparison — depth trumps breadth. The representativeness of the following analysis is thus something of an unavoidably open question, although much of what I argue resonates with the existing literature on the police.

Ethnography involves not only the collection of data through observations and conversations but also the analysis of the resulting field notes. In my case, the analysis consisted of attempts to order what I witnessed, to explain how the territorial actions I observed were structured. My analysis unearthed six normative orders as the most significant factors in shaping how officers make and mark space. This, then, might be called an "analytic ethnography,"[4] the development of a framework for explicating social action.

This book is intended as a contribution to a number of disciplines. Geographers will find rich support for their oft-stated insistence on the importance of spatiality for social action in general, and for the exercise of power in particular. Sociologists will learn something about the exercise of state power and about organizational dynamics. Students of the police will develop a fuller appreciation of the importance of territoriality for policing and also see the main motivations of police behavior laid out in a clear and systematic fashion. And those interested in matters urban will learn how and why police power is inserted within the fabric of the city. Given this broad intended audience, I at times review material that will be well known to some of my readers. I ask forbearance in these situations and trust that the analysis and empirical material will ultimately prove worth the wait.

My analysis includes several examples of police territoriality and explains that territoriality by elucidating the six normative orders that structure it. The first chapter pursues two goals: to explain the significance of competent territorial action for state agents such as the police, and to conceptualize fully the term *normative order.* With this theoretical apparatus in place, attention is turned briefly, in chapter 2, to a description of the field site and the research conducted there, and then, in chapters 3 through 8, to substantive attempts to define each of the six normative orders and to explain their shaping influence on police territoriality. Chapter 9 concludes the analysis with a discussion of the relationships between the six normative orders and a review of the lessons of this work for the study of the state, territoriality, and the police.

1. TERRITORIALITY
AND THE POLICE

THE INTERSECTION OF FLORENCE AND Normandie Avenues is now world famous as the "flashpoint" of the 1992 civil unrest in Los Angeles. It was the scene of the brutal beating of trucker Reginald Denny, and of a general mayhem that reputedly spread from there to the rest of South Central Los Angeles. Born at Florence and Normandie, the common narrative holds, a contagion of anarchy engulfed surrounding neighborhoods in chaos and destruction.

Despite the seeming logic of this narrative, however, significant unrest occurred earlier elsewhere,[1] and it is not clear why Florence and Normandie has become the vaunted flashpoint of the events that followed.[2]

To explain the importance of this particular intersection, it helps to recall what occurred there before Denny was beaten. A large contingent from the Los Angeles Police Department not only failed to stem the unrest, but actually *left the scene.* This retreat later represented to commentators the crucial point at which the forces of disorder won an important victory. In the absence of police-enforced coercive sanctions, people vented their anger and disaffection freely. That the LAPD lost the battle at Florence and Normandie and eventually secured order only with massive help from the National Guard was seen as serious enough to warrant an independent commission — headed by former FBI and CIA chief William Webster — to investigate the department's "unusual occurrence" strategy.

The saga of Florence and Normandie reveals a core public expectation of the police — that officers can, when necessary, secure control of the flow of action in space. The police, in other words, are expected to be effective agents of territoriality, to be able to control social action by controlling area.[3] Indeed, the Webster Commission faulted the LAPD for not adopting more effective geopolitical strategies. According to the commission's report, the LAPD should have sealed perimeters around areas of turmoil and then "sectored" those areas into units "that could be taken back one by one."[4] This was advice the LAPD took seriously. Shortly after the unrest, the department instituted mandatory training for all officers in "mobile field tactics," a series of coordinated maneuvers designed to enable them to respond swiftly and seal areas of disorder.

The Police and Territoriality

The dramatic images of LAPD officers scurrying from Florence and Normandie represented their failure at sociospatial control. This should not occur: the police are expected, when they are summoned, to exercise their coercive power to secure control over space. In fact, control of space is a fundament of overall police efforts at social control. This is most dramatically obvious in technologically sophisticated forces such as the LAPD, during a vehicle pursuit like the one I described in the Introduction. Elaborate communications and transportation technologies are trained on a target; the suspect is marked, monitored, contained, and captured.

But spatial control is just as important and obvious in more mundane order-maintenance activities. Officers typically bring domestic and business disputes under control by segregating the combatants and often by convincing at least one party to leave the scene. They end loud parties by sending people home. They regularly sweep gang members from street corners, underage youths from saloons, prostitutes from the fronts of cheap motels, homeless people from commercial thoroughfares. Further, one of their most potent means of exercising control is to jail, an especially severe territorial act—a suspect is transported from one place and confined to another. Simply put, many police strategies to create public order involve enacting boundaries and restricting access; police power rests upon a political geography.[5] As one officer said about his strategies for a house where drugs were sold, "Basically I do whatever I can to get them to move along."

As Sack makes clear, social power relies fundamentally upon territoriality.[6] It is certainly the case that the police would be largely impotent without the capacity to create and enforce boundaries, to restrict people's mobility in and around certain areas. The amateur videotape of the police fleeing from Florence and Normandie was replayed incessantly on Los Angeles television, the images shocking evidence of the inability of the police to secure order through securing space.

Bittner and the Neglected Significance of Territoriality

One way of demonstrating the importance of territoriality to the police is through an examination of the influential work of Egon Bittner, who tried to explain the central role of the police in society.[7] Bittner's argument, while nuanced, is ultimately quite straightforward: that the capacity to use force is the core of the police role. The police are summoned to situations in which the use of force is or might be necessary. He makes this argument by describing a series of situations in which people had "called the cops." What is initially striking about these vignettes, Bittner suggests, is that they are quite dissimilar. The cases are worth repeating: a woman is upset about a man visiting her maid in the maid's quarters; a nurse is concerned about children in their grandmother's dilapidated apartment; a man is corralled because he fits the description of a wanted suspect; two ambulance attendants need help convincing a sick man to go to the hospital; youths are fixing cars and drinking beer on a city street; a couple is quarreling in an apartment.[8]

Bittner unifies these disparate stories by explaining that in each case the cops were called because of their *capacity* to use force; in each case, those who summoned the police believed that the situation was such that force might have been needed to effect the desired outcome. It is not the reality of the use of force that for Bittner is the crucial factor, but the capacity to use force. The police, for Bittner, are most basically understood as an agency that stands ready to use force and can influence action because of that potential.

Although Weber's name is never mentioned in Bittner's discussion, a Weberian spirit seems to animate it. In particular, it is Weber's definition of the state that appears to undergird Bittner's argument. Weber defines the state as the "political grouping that maintains the legitimate capacity to use force."[9] As agents of state law, the police are the social agency charged with the capacity to use force legitimately.

What is of interest is Bittner's failure to consider the rest of Weber's definition of the state, which includes an explicit territorial component. It is not just the legitimate use of force that makes the state unique, but also the use of that force across a specifically defined territory. This aspect of Weber's definition moves us toward an appreciation for the importance of territoriality to the police; state control, in the modern era, contains an explicit need to secure boundedness, to make the state's boundaries clear and valent. One aspect of this control is pointed outward—thus the importance for Weber and various political sociologists following in his footsteps of the military as a key facet of modern state power.[10] The other aspect is pointed inward, toward what Giddens terms "internal pacification,"[11] the capacity of the state to exercise regularized control of its subject population. It is here that police power becomes crucial.

This is all rather abstract. It is fruitful to return to Bittner's vignettes and note that while force is not used in any of the situations, *territoriality* is. In each case, the police remove people from one location and place them in another. In each case, successful resolution of the problem requires denying people access to one area or coercing them into another or both. In other words, the processes of internal pacification so central to the authority of the modern state readily depend on the capacity of the police to mark and enact meaningful boundaries, to restrict people's capacity to act by regulating their movements in space.

Weber, Foucault, and the Microgeopolitics of State Power

Two strands of recent work draw attention to the relationship between state power and territoriality. One, drawing upon Weber, describes the modern state as a bureaucratic administration impelled toward extensive control of the people and activities within its circumscribed territory. Another derives from Foucault, who discussed the investment of power in wider and finer fashion via territorial tactics and spatialized categories. These works have important differences, but both stress the spatiality of modern power and thus represent instructive places to begin an investigation of police territoriality.

Weber

Weber's interest in territorial control inheres in his definition of the state. The state, for Weber, is a compulsory political association that upholds its claim to legitimate force to enforce order within its territory. Further, the state establishes an organized administration to enforce its order. Weber's approach thus emphasizes the state's bureaucratic institutions and their development in tandem with territorial boundedness. As Mann puts it, boundaries "derive from an emergent need to institutionalize social relations."[12] The modern state is unique in its institutionalization and its boundedness, and therefore differs radically from the less-centralized and vaguely circumscribed political entities that preceded it. The state's explicit territorial delimitation separates it from other powerful social institutions. No group within civil society is similarly delimited, and thus none possesses the mandate to organize such activities as taxation, conscription, or public order.[13]

The demarcation of boundaries is a prevalent theme in discussions of the modern state as an administrative unit[14] and as a nation.[15] The boundary differentiates inside and outside, which assists the state's attempt to create a sense of nationhood and defines its range of administrative concern. These administrative responsibilities compose the realm of infrastructural power, the capacity, in Giddens's terms, to "influence even the most intimate features of daily activity."[16]

This capacity relies upon surveillance, the state's ability to collect, store, and use information regarding its citizens. This connects to Weber's concern with the implementation and enforcement of legal rules over the state's territory,[17] which, Dandeker asserts, "involves a permanent and continuous exercise of surveillance."[18]

These general insights link the exercise of modern state power with the surveillance and control of space and thus are instructive for an understanding of police territoriality. These formulations importantly address territoriality at the theoretical level and thereby avoid merely relegating issues of space to the concrete, contingent level.[19] Spatial control is so crucial to the modern state that ineffective territoriality means, simply, incomplete state power. The focus on "internal pacification" also matches historical narratives of modern policing, which stress how the chaos of nineteenth-century cities created concern about disorder and crime and spurred the creation of formalized, state-sponsored police forces.[20] These forces were largely designed to preserve boundaries between social groups in the thickly mixed spaces of the early-industrial city. In addition, the growth of bureaucratic practices underlay the spread of police forces throughout the United States and helped bolster the legitimacy of the police.[21] Many early American police forces were accused of corruption and inefficiency, and reformers used bureaucratic and legalized rules to control and legitimate the police.[22]

Although Weberian-inspired work reveals the territorial underpinnings of the modern state and the elaborate bureaucratic structures that sustain that geopolitical power, it cannot provide a full understanding of police territoriality for three reasons. First, the preeminent concern is with the state's center and the practices and ideologies developed there. While it is important, such a focus can overlook the complicated politics of implementing policy at the periphery. There is always the possibility that the state's power, exercised at its extremities, will escape its formalized bureaucratic procedures. Also, space is implicitly understood to be undifferentiated in these center-focused analyses. The challenges that different localities pose to the implementation of centrally produced laws are therefore ignored.[23]

Second, Weberian work can overemphasize the rational character of state bureaucracy. Although surveillance and control require formalized procedures, less rational impulses also structure state behavior. Weber sought to describe a variety of rationalities that determine human action, but, when discussing modern bureaucratized society, emphasized purposively rational action and downplayed normative or affectual action.[24] As a result, the multiple contexts of state action are often excluded from a Weberian framework that emphasizes rationality.[25] For instance, it is clear from several ethnographic analyses that bureaucratic structures do not exclusively determine police behavior.[26] As a result, other factors must figure in explanations of police territoriality. In particular, investigations must include an examination of how the cultures of enforcement agencies shape how the formalized impulses of control are actually practiced. Further, these cultures of enforcement will vary from place to place, given the unique historical development of each agency of sociospatial control. Los Angeles, for example, developed a particular brand of policing that emphasized technological sophistication and aggressive patrolling.

Finally, the discussions of territoriality are not well developed empirically. The stress on the importance of territorial control is well taken, but the processes of state territoriality are not fully investigated. Without a more empirically rich investigation of actual territorial practices, a complete picture of state territoriality is unattainable.

Foucault

The relationship between knowledge, power, and space in modern surveillance was also important to Foucault, who documented the diffusion of the disciplinary network in finer and wider realms. He urged a look away from the center to the periphery, where power worked in a disjointed and multifaceted way. Foucault was less concerned with the formalized procedures that create and legitimate disciplinary power and focused instead on power's specific techniques at its extremities. In his analysis, spatial matters figured large. He not only discussed the intensity and extension of discipline with such geopolitical metaphors as battle and tactics but also described how discipline marks and controls populations in space.[27]

Foucault provides an important antidote to the Weberian tendency to stress the center by encouraging ascending analyses up from the periphery, analyses that focus explicitly on the "how" of power. His discussions of the relationship between territorial markings and social control have spurred a number of insightful investigations into the means by which various subject populations are emplaced within cartographies of power.[28] It is certainly true that the LAPD and other police agencies employ a number of knowledge bases and technologically sophisticated techniques to locate, monitor, and control the citizenry. However, a too-ready acceptance of Foucault's analytics obscures a full understanding of police territoriality.

The primary issues here are Foucault's overweening emphasis on power and his related unwillingness to sociologize the workings of discipline.[29] For instance, Foucault downplays the role of the state and its legal order, and thus fails to develop an appreciation for the fundamental intertwining of state power and discipline.[30] Also, the variety of social impulses lying behind such an instance of modern discipline as police territoriality cannot be captured with a strong Foucauldian emphasis on power.[31]

In sum, Weberian and Foucauldian works provide important insights into modern power and its investment in territorial practice: they reveal the spatial foundations of modern social control, and they draw attention to both the formalized practices of the state and the actual practice of territorial power at the state's extremities. However, these works provide little insight into the less-formalized impulses that structure police territoriality. The concept of normative order provides a more satisfactory route for understanding how the LAPD and other police agencies make and mark space.

Normative Orders and State Action

A persistent weakness of social-structural work is that it typically neglects the workings of culture. The abstract formulations that describe the economy or the state often fail to recognize how cultural understandings underwrite the production and reproduction of such structures.[32] Conversely, culture theorists often neglect the social forces that create and sustain cultural understandings; culture sometimes appears as a realm divorced from any social moorings.[33] These lines of thought make clear the need to treat society and culture as mutually determined and interpellated. In terms of the police, this means recognizing how the "structural" realms of law and bureaucracy are rife with cultural meanings. Within the world of the police, there are cultural codes that are both dependent on and independent of law and bureaucracy, and they deeply infuse the daily practices of patrol. Police territoriality, in other words, is practiced according to normative orders that mix the social-structural and the cultural.

These normative orders consist of rules and practices that structure action. Further, these orders center on a primary value, and thereby provide meaning for behavior. The concept of normative order thus captures the cognitive and the affectual, the rules that people follow and the meanings they create.

The term *normative order* is most often associated with Parsons, who strongly emphasized the role of norms and values in regulating human behavior.[34] My usage of the term, however, differs from Parsons's. I include rules in the definition, to underscore the importance of the acquisition and use of cognitive understandings in the conduct of everyday action. This is related to a stronger emphasis on the reflexivity of human actors than Parsons's schema allowed. Actors, in other words, are not "cultural dopes" who unconsciously internalize value structures and act accordingly, but are active agents who apply cognitive understandings to new situations.[35] As we will see, police officers constantly work to develop definitions of the situations they encounter, to match the events they witness to a relevant ordering scheme. There are different schemes available to police officers, however, and thus the processes by which situations are defined and controlled are potentially a source of conflict. This contrasts with the primary thrust of Parsonian work, which underscores the importance of value internalization as a means to minimize conflict.

At the same time, I wish to highlight, with Parsons, the important role of values in providing meaning for actions, and thus for motivating actors to abide by rules. It is easier, for example, to convince officers to walk flush against buildings on dangerous calls if they are reminded that such action might guarantee their safety. The rule is wedded to the value of the sanctity of life, and thereby carries more potency.

My definition of normative order thus ties together rules

and values; it acknowledges the reflexivity in human action without minimizing the important motivating aspect of matters of affectual significance. It also helps relate structure and action by capturing the ordering function of rules and the practices they engender. However, agents possess a capacity to transform these orders by transposing them to new situations;[36] as a result, the reproduction of each normative order is a contingent outcome of ongoing human action.

A further advantage of this approach, as I indicated earlier, is its implicit pluralistic view of society and culture. In other words, neither society nor culture is understood as a seamless whole, but instead as multiple, fragmented, and conflictual.[37] Different normative orders structure our worlds, and these orders do not always cohere. As a result, political tension is an endemic fact of social life. This is clearly the case in organizations such as the LAPD, where normative orders constantly abut. The normative order of bureaucratic control, for example, often explicitly contrasts with that of adventure/machismo and creates an interminable conflict between supervisors interested in a smooth flow of command and patrol officers anxious to hunt suspects at the whim of their instincts. This tension between orders introduces another realm in which human agency and reflexivity become important; when orders conflict, actors must decide which receives priority. This further complicates the reproduction of any normative order.

Society, Culture, and Space

Just as social-structural works often neglect the shaping influence of culture, they also regularly overlook the spatial embeddedness of social action.[38] Social action always occurs in place, and thus is shaped by spatial contexts. At the same time, places themselves are always socially—and culturally—

constructed. The social, the cultural, and the spatial are thereby deeply intertwined. Analysis of everyday police behavior, in other words, must pay attention not only to its social and cultural construction, but also to its intractable spatiality; in working to uphold socially constructed notions of public order, officers define and seek to control the spaces they patrol. Police officers so fundamentally embed their power in the boundaries they create and enforce that analysis of their practices must attend to the means by which they make and mark space.

The context of police encounters shapes how officers choose to act.[39] Officers often read situations against their understandings of what is normal or typical for the location; how they interpret action is shaped by *where* it occurs. This observation accords with broader insights into the influence of place on human actors. Understandings of place commonly shape how people interpret the nature and motivation of action. These geographic understandings are important elements in the narratives we construct about behavior.[40] Place is not just a neutral backdrop, but an important element structuring the nature and comprehension of social action.

For police officers, the location of a given action shapes how they understand what is transpiring and how they should respond. Therefore, it is important to discern how they socially construct the areas they patrol, to determine how various normative orders shape how officers make space. For example, the normative order of safety leads officers to differentiate areas as either "pro-police" or "anti-police." As the terms suggest, officers feel free from threat in the former and dangerously vulnerable in the latter. They will thereby be more suspicious of actors in anti-police areas than in pro-police ones, and are more likely to respond aggressively to challenges to their authority in anti-police areas. The preexisting definition of a space as either safe or dangerous crucially affects how officers behave there.[41]

The manner in which police officers make space clearly influences how they mark it. The nature and range of territorial tactics officers will deploy are contingent upon how they define the space they are confronting. Those tactics are further contingent upon what goal the officers are pursuing. An officer seeking to demonstrate bravery and adventurousness, for example, may enact territorial strategies different from those employed by an officer most interested in securing the safety of all the parties involved. Different normative orders, in other words, define different territorial strategies to achieve the relevant goal. Regardless of the goal, however, territoriality is a basic strategy that officers employ to secure public order; successful marking of space is a foundation of successful policing.

The processes by which officers make and mark space are basic components of the exercise of police power. The struggle to define and control place is one that police officers, like other agents of the state, engage in daily, often against active resistance.[42] Cultural conceptions of space and place are central components of political struggles, because to dictate the nature of space and the action that occurs there is to exercise tremendous power.[43] For police officers interested in creating public order, the control of space is crucial. Without such control, police agencies stand to suffer the public embarrassment inflicted upon the LAPD by the videotape of its retreat from Florence and Normandie.

Conclusion

The normative orders that structure police practice shape the processes by which officers define and seek to control space. Two of these orders—the law and bureaucratic control—largely define space *for* the officers and constitute more formalized and structural systems. These more "objective" orders, however, are supplemented by four others—adventure/machismo, safety, competence, and morality—that also structure the practices of police territoriality. These orders are constructed within the subcultural world of the officers and thus infuse the more objective realms of law and bureaucracy with potent subjective elements. The more formalized impulses and practices of state territoriality are not, in other words, applied unproblematically to the social landscape, but are augmented and influenced by subcultural considerations. These subcultural factors are, in turn, shaped by the historical circumstances unique to a given police force.

The burden of the rest of my analysis is to demonstrate the analytic value of the concept of normative order, to demonstrate how the concept significantly illumines our understanding of how and why the police act to control people by controlling territory. Each order consists of rules and practices that shape how officers make and mark space, how they define the areas they patrol and enact boundaries to secure control. Although the orders differ in their scope and power, each is influential in determining how officers create and enact space.

The analysis that follows brings together concepts that are frequently opposed in social geographic analysis: objective and subjective; state and society; society and space; politics and culture. And, importantly, I aspire not only to theoretical clarity and acuity, but also to a demonstrable understanding of the practices of human agents daily engaged in an attempt to secure order through securing space.

This challenge will be forestalled for a chapter, however. I need first to describe the setting in which the research took place and to describe the nature of the research itself.

2. THE SETTING AND THE RESEARCH

THE WILSHIRE DIVISION IS ONE of eighteen patrol divisions of the Los Angeles Police Department (see Map 1). It encompasses an area of about six square miles. The northern boundary is Beverly Boulevard. For most of the division, the eastern boundary is Normandie Avenue, the southern boundary the Santa Monica Freeway, and the western boundary La Cienega Boulevard. The southwest portion of the division, an irregularly shaped area south of the Santa Monica Freeway, is an exception to those boundaries (see Map 2).

The social landscape of the Wilshire Division is tremendously varied. There is a significant mix of commercial and residential areas, and of different social groups. Commercial activities are concentrated on Wilshire, Pico, Fairfax, and other busy streets. The range and value of commercial establishments vary considerably, from the tall towers of finance along Wilshire to the ramshackle liquor stores in the southern end

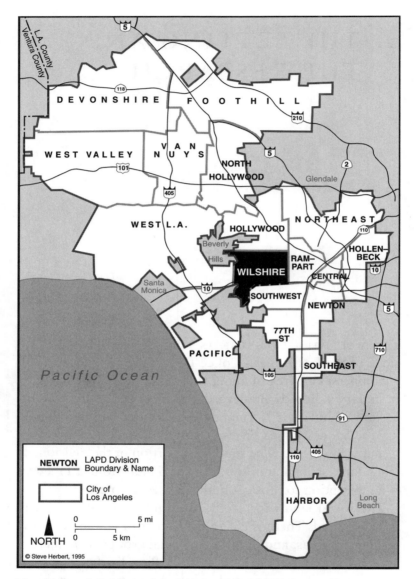

Map 1. Patrol divisions of the Los Angeles Police Department

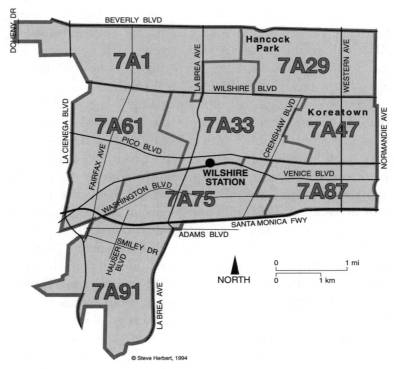

Map 2. The Wilshire Division

of the division, along, for example, Washington Boulevard. Residential areas are similarly mixed, from dense apartment buildings in the northeast part of the division to the spacious single-family homes of Hancock Park in the north central area. Most other areas of the division are a mix of single- and multiple-family dwellings.

In general, housing values decrease as one moves from the west to the east in the division, and, even more significantly, from the north to the south. This spatial patterning of housing values mimics that of white settlement. The northwest area of the division has census tracts with percentages of white residents as high as 92. The white percentage of one tract in the southeast, however, is only 1.4. Blacks live primarily in the south and somewhat to the east. Latinos and Asians share the northeast area, known as Koreatown. The Latino population remains fairly high in the east central area, but is minimal farther west and south.

The Wilshire Division, not surprisingly, is touted within the Los Angeles Police Department as a good place to learn how to become a police officer because of its demographic variety. Wilshire officers are certain to be busy because they work one of the most crime-prone divisions in the city. As Table 2 illustrates, the Wilshire Division ranked in the top four divisions citywide in the incidence of each of five major crimes in 1993; it was first in robbery and auto theft, second in rape, third in burglary, and fourth in homicide. Needless to say, the division's totals were much higher than the average in each category. For the sake of comparison, Table 2 includes the highest and lowest division totals for each crime. The table makes it easier to understand why Wilshire officers complained regularly about an excessive workload.

The division has its own station, located near the center, where officers gather before each shift, meet for roll call, and are dispatched in their patrol cars. Each roll call is supervised by a watch commander, who usually holds the rank of lieutenant. There are three main watches. Morning watch runs from 11:00 P.M. to 7:45 A.M., day watch from 7:00 A.M. to 3:45 P.M., and night watch from 3:00 to 11:45 P.M. Five to seven two-person patrol cars and two to four patrol supervisors, who hold the rank of sergeant, are assigned to each watch. These three primary watches are supplemented by two smaller watches—midday, which runs from 10:00 A.M. to 6:45 P.M., and midnight, which runs from 6:00 P.M. to 2:45 A.M. These midwatches typically include two or three patrol cars and a single sergeant as supervisor.

Table 2. Reported crimes in the Wilshire Division, 1993

	Number	Rank	High	Low	Average
Homicide	77	4	151	9	59
Rape	132	2	173	41	99
Robbery	3,856	1	3,856	977	2,120
Burglary	4,067	3	4,345	1,896	3,209
Auto theft	6,238	1	6,238	1,526	4,157

The watch commander has primary responsibility for patrol during each watch. The watch commander does, however, have two superiors within the division. The first is the
patrol captain, who is responsible for the overall patrol op-
eration through all watches. The second is the area captain,
who is responsible for all operations in the division, which
include not only patrol but also detectives, vice, and the senior lead officers. The latter group is responsible for community relations and for addressing ongoing problems that
require sustained attention that patrol officers cannot provide.

Patrol cars are usually assigned to one of the division's seven
Basic Car Areas (see Map 2), the LAPD equivalent of "beats."
Each Basic Car Area is patrolled by a two-officer team in a
single car. Optimally, each Basic Car will be assigned all of
the calls in its area. The department officially hopes that
each patrol officer will work in a single area, both within
and across watches, the better to understand that area. In
practice, however, this goal is not met. The heavy call load
in Wilshire means that each car is assigned calls throughout
the division, and the general shortage of patrol officers means
that, given days off and vacations, it is hard for watch commanders to preserve "Basic Car integrity," that is, to consistently assign officers to the same car.

The Basic Car patrol officers are immediately supervised by
patrol sergeants. Optimally, there are three or four sergeants

on each watch. During my fieldwork period, however, it was not uncommon for there to be only one or two. Further, paper work often keeps sergeants inside. On patrol, sergeants respond to calls for various reasons: when they are requested; when the danger to patrol officers is high; when they fear officers are in a situation that could result in a lawsuit from a citizen; when they wish to watch a particular officer at work; when the call seems interesting to them; and, during my fieldwork, when they thought the call would be interesting to me.

In addition to the patrol officers and their supervising sergeants, a "special problems" unit typically patrols during evening watch. Officially called the Community Response Unit (CRU), the unit selects problem areas for ongoing surveillance. CRU cars are expected to avoid responding to radio calls and are assigned to particular parts of the division in hopes of stemming particular crimes. For example, CRU cars were deployed one night in the east central part of the division, where a large number of Honda automobiles had recently been stolen; the officers were to investigate each Honda they saw for evidence that it might have been stolen. Typically, three or four CRU cars work a given night, supervised by a sergeant devoted solely to CRU.

The Wilshire Division includes several operations in addition to basic patrol and patrol-related functions. Each Basic Car Area not only has a patrol car assigned to it for each watch (at least optimally), but also has a senior lead officer. Each SLO has three primary responsibilities. The first is to maintain close relations with community groups in the area. This means, principally, helping to form and maintain neighborhood watch groups but can also mean meeting with business groups, school groups, and so on. The second responsibility is to monitor ongoing crime problems or situations deemed to be criminological. For example, SLOs will maintain regular surveillance on sites known as drug sales locations, buildings prone to graffiti, and vacant lots used by homeless people as campsites. The third, in conjunction with the second, is to apprise officers working the Basic Car of situations that require ongoing surveillance.

The senior lead officers are not officially considered a component of patrol. Their direct supervisor is a sergeant assigned to the Senior Lead Office who reports directly to the area captain. That sergeant is also responsible for the two division foot beats, one of which patrols the eastern end of Wilshire Boulevard, the other parts of Koreatown. The foot beats patrol during the day and are responsible primarily for maintaining public order in these two areas, both of which house a large number of commercial establishments. This means, in practice, trying to keep the areas clear of homeless people, street vendors, drunks, and others about whom business owners complain.

Besides the Basic Cars and the SLOs, the area captain also supervises the detectives and the vice unit. Each of these groups has its own primary supervisor; in the case of the detectives the supervisor is a lieutenant; the vice supervisor is a sergeant. Narcotics officers and officers from the gang unit, CRASH (Community Resources Against Street Hoodlums), also work in the Wilshire Division, but they are supervised at the bureau level. Four patrol bureaus—South, Central, West, and Valley—exist in the LAPD's organizational chart, and each contains four or five of the eighteen patrol divisions. The Wilshire Division is one of four divisions located in West Bureau. Each bureau is supervised by a deputy chief. As a result, the Wilshire area captain does not have direct supervisory control over the CRASH and narcotics operations that take place within the division.

Thus, on any given night, a variety of personnel may be deployed throughout the division. Basic patrol units are sure to be "out amongst 'em," but so may be various CRU cars and CRASH officers. SLOs may be attending a neighborhood watch meeting or patrolling and repatrolling the two or three major problems in their areas. Narcotics officers may be engaged in buy-bust operations or monitoring situations for future operations. And a variety of outside units may be called in when necessary: not only patrol units from other divisions, but also the helicopters from Air Support or the dogs from K-9.[1]

This should not give the impression that the division is necessarily well patrolled. During my fieldwork, there were many instances when the full complement of patrol cars was not deployed, when the helicopter and K-9 units did not respond when requested, when SLOs complained about their inability to get narcotics officers to "work" an area, when CRU cars were forced, because of the heavy call load, to abandon their special projects and respond to radio calls. Though the LAPD network can be impressively wide and varied, it is infrequently developed to its fullest extent in any given area at any given time.

The Research

My analysis draws upon fieldwork conducted within the Wilshire Division between August 1993 and March 1994. The fieldwork consisted mostly of my accompanying an officer during his or her shift. I did my largest number of ride-alongs, thirty-five, with patrol supervisors, that is, sergeants assigned to monitor the work of the officers in the Basic Cars. These ride-alongs averaged six hours in length, and I attended roll call as part of half of them. In addition, I accompanied senior lead officers on twenty occasions, which typically included patrolling those areas of most concern to them. These ride-alongs averaged four hours. I also spent four evenings in the Communications Division watching the dispatchers for Wilshire Division assign calls; walked each of the Wilshire Division foot beats once with the responsible officers; rode twice in an Air Support helicopter; spent a full watch with West Bureau CRASH sergeants on a night in which their officers worked in the Wilshire Division; and observed two division "training days." The first of these training days, developed by the department's psychological services staff, involved a third of the division's personnel in an airing of their grievances. The second, developed by several patrol sergeants, involved a series of tactical exercises on the grounds of the now-abandoned Ambassador Hotel.

I carried a small spiral notebook to jot down brief notations of incidents as they occurred. Within twenty-four hours of each observation, I typed up much longer and more fully developed notes describing each incident and how the officers responded to it. I also recorded key elements of conversations either between myself and an officer or officers or between officers. By the end of the fieldwork, I had recorded nearly four hundred single-spaced pages of field notes. These field notes are the principal source for my analysis.

The Los Angeles Police Department was a highly politicized organization at the time of the fieldwork. I entered the field just four months after the conclusion of the second trial of LAPD officers involved in the beating of Rodney King, which capped a two-year period of intense public scrutiny of the department. I was also, as far as I am aware, the first social scientist allowed to do extensive ethnographic work in the LAPD in nearly fifteen years. As a result, I fully expected to be welcomed with less than open arms.

On the whole, however, the members of the division that I encountered were helpful and forthcoming. A few officers were unresponsive when I initiated conversations, but the vast majority were friendly and willing to talk openly about their work. With about six officers I developed a particularly strong rapport and was able to explore issues in somewhat greater depth with them. I learned quickly that officers were occasionally suspicious of some questions but would readily discuss the incidents that they handled. Frustrations with the department or the public, or more personal feelings about the work, were not readily elicited via direct questions but emerged around the edges of conversations about events.[2]

I formally interviewed only three officers. These interviews occurred during the last few weeks of the fieldwork and taught me little that I had not already learned from my many informal conversations. On the one hand, I was disappointed that the interviews were not more productive. On the other hand, they made clear that my earlier, less formal conversations had taught me much.

The chapters that follow evolved from my lengthy and recurrent reviews of my fieldnotes. My analysis represents a clear process of interpreting a cultural system and emerges from a sustained engagement with the thoughts and practices of the agents of that system. Thus, while the language is my own, and while the capacity of outsiders to understand a cultural system is always inherently limited, I am confident that my story would be recognizable to those about whom I write.[3]

We are now in a position to begin more extensive investigations of the six normative orders that structure police territoriality. The most expansive of these is the law, the subject of chapter 3.

3. THE LAW
AND POLICE
TERRITORIALITY

POLICE RESEARCHERS HISTORICALLY HAVE DEVOTED much attention to the issue of discretion. Many early and influential analyses of the police demonstrated that, regardless of what legal or bureaucratic regulations might stipulate, police officers possess considerable autonomy in the field.[1] According to this line of thought, legal and bureaucratic dictates are neither unambiguous nor capable of covering all possible contingencies. Further, officers are not directly supervised during most incidents. As a result, considerable variability is introduced into modern policing.

Various factors—the time of day, the personal characteristics of individual officers, the nature of the call for service, the demeanor of complainant and suspect—seem to condition police discretion.[2] The location of the incident is also recognized as crucial, because it may shape how officers view situations;[3] officers may understand an area to be characterized by a certain way of life that must be taken into consideration. For example, Bittner's well-known analysis revealed that officers are deeply aware of the transient nature of social life on skid row and take that into account in making decisions about whether and how to intervene.[4] This is in keeping with Banton's broader argument that police officers are acutely aware of the prevailing moral order in the areas they patrol and act in accordance more with that order than with the law.[5]

Indeed, the literature on police discretion consistently downplays the law as a principal determinant of police behavior. Law is rather seen as a resource for officers, allowing them enough leeway to justify whatever actions they choose, for whatever reason, to undertake.[6] The enforcement of law is thus colored by a variety of extralegal considerations, many of them involving the particular characteristics of the locales where the police intervene.

This line of argument has, in a somewhat different vein, been explored by geographers interested in the relationships between law and space.[7] Such work draws inspiration from critical legal scholars who argue that the law is not univocal and abstract, but is rather an ongoing work of interpretation and thus subject to a variety of social and political influences.[8] The argument that society and law are mutually constituted moves easily, for geographers, into an argument that space and law are similarly interlaced; like society, space is not a passive substrate awaiting the external molding agent of law but a fundamental constituent in the creation and implementation of law. Not only does law help produce space by defining it and stipulating what can and cannot occur within it,[9] but its enforcement and interpretation are influenced by socially held ideas about space and by material spatial contexts. In the case of police officers, the realities of the neighborhoods they patrol and their conceptions of the nature of social life in those areas can significantly influence whether and how they enforce the law.

Despite the existence of police discretion and the undoubted significance of geographical variation in conditioning that discretion, however, it is important not to lose sight of the importance of law to the practices of the police. No matter how regularly police officers may escape the control of the formal strictures of the law, their basic mission, responsibilities, and powers are principally defined by legal stipulations.[10] Laws define the crimes the police are responsible for detecting, the techniques they are permitted to use, the parameters and limits of their potential intervention into social life. In terms of police territoriality, the law helps define the aims of territorial actions and defines where and how the police can legally act territorially. Although space may help determine how the law is enforced by conditioning police discretion, it is nonetheless true that law helps to create a geography for police officers by delimiting those spaces where they can intervene and the permissible range of actions within those spaces. For example, the law provides a critical distinction between public and private space that has tremendous ramifications for police actions.

It is not just that the law is important to the police, of course, but also that the police are of fundamental importance in the maintenance of the law. Indeed, for Weber, the legal order is a unique social order because it is "externally guaranteed by the probability that coercion to bring about conformity will be applied by a staff of people holding themselves specially ready for that purpose."[11] The police obviously constitute such a staff and are thus a key agency involved in securing the legally — and administratively — defined order of the state. The police are thus both enmeshed within and

protective of the state's legal order; the law and the police enable one another.

It is the main contention of this chapter that any thorough understanding of police territoriality must include an
examination of the ways in which law structures police practices. I demonstrate how law defines the crimes to which the
police respond, the geographic parameters around particular permissible actions, and the range of permissible and required territorial practices. These clusters of legal regulations
significantly condition the territorial actions police officers
regularly undertake to enforce public order. As I make clear,
however, legal regulations do not *determine* police actions.
The boundary between public and private space, for example, is not always clearly fixed; as I demonstrate, its permeability varies situationally and thus does not necessarily constrain officers in advance in all cases. Further, there is no easy
means to predict just how faithful officers will be to strict
legal regulations. My claims, therefore, are somewhat mod-
est: that officers often take legal rules seriously, and that these
rules shape the exercise of police territoriality. I show later
in the chapter, and in other chapters, that legal rules do not
confine officers in all cases.

Although any number of different values are invoked or
protected by the law, for the police it is the law itself that
emerges as a central value. More specifically, enforcement
of the law is regularly invoked as a (perhaps *the*) principal
function of the police in society and serves as a powerful legitimating force for police advocates.[12] This value of law enforcement, however, is not solely hollow ideology; as we
will see, officers regularly view situations through the prism
of law to decide whether and how they should act, perhaps
aware at some level that their legitimacy depends in part upon
abiding by legal prescriptions.

Thus, law constitutes a normative order for police territoriality by defining a range of rules and permissible practices organized around a central value—the enforcement of law—that provides significant meaning for police behavior. The law is thus important in shaping daily police practices, even if it often conflicts with the imperatives of other normative orders.

The remainder of the chapter explores these points. In the next section I discuss the role of law in defining certain actions as crimes and, as such, worthy of a response from the police. Further, to the extent that the law defines crimes, it helps the police socially construct the spaces they patrol. One way LAPD officers differentiate the various Basic Car Areas is in terms of the most common crimes found there, and therefore the type of patrol challenges they will encounter.

I then move to a discussion of the salient spatial parameters defined for the police by the law. Most significant here is the distinction between public and private space. These parameters have very real consequences for the actions of the officers because the range of permissible police responses to an incident is shaped by *where* the incident occurs. Importantly, the line between public and private space is not always fixed, and officers may sometimes transcend the line. Further, the boundary is not always just a restriction on police action but can be mobilized to accomplish some larger public aim, such as clearing space of transients.

In the last section I counterbalance any tendency to overstate the importance of law in determining police territorial practice. The discussion demonstrates how legally permissible actions are not always taken by police, even in the face of blatant criminal activity, and how some actions are taken without clear, defensible legal grounds. This provides an opening for consideration of the conditioning of other normative orders on the practices of police territoriality in subsequent chapters.

Legal Definitions

As analysts of police discretion suggest, legal regulations do
not determine police practice; a variety of extralegal considerations come into play in the majority of police actions.
Nonetheless, the law is a very real presence in ongoing police
practice. The law serves as an ever-present prism through
which officers view the situations they encounter. Officers
often measure an incident against the legal definition of what
constitutes a crime. This is a primary means by which officers define a situation, and it significantly affects their subsequent response.

Defining Crimes

*A slow weekday afternoon is interrupted when the sergeant is
called to the scene of a domestic dispute. A woman is claiming
that her husband is threatening her with a metal pipe. A patrol
car visited the scene earlier in the afternoon, but made no arrest. Frustrated, the woman is now threatening a lawsuit if the
officers do not act decisively.*

*Three patrol car teams are on the scene when the sergeant
arrives. An obviously intoxicated man is sitting in front of the
apartment building and is being questioned by several of the
officers. He is the husband in question. His wife, who is inside,
claims that, once drunk, her husband began tearing up the
apartment and threatening violence. The officers, however, find
evidence of neither disruption nor physical abuse. They huddle
in front of the apartment building and discuss the situation.
Their only possible arrest, they reason, is for drunkenness in
public. They recognize, however, that the man is only in public
because the first officers on the scene ordered him out of the
apartment to create a measure of calm. Because he lives in the
apartment, his right to be there is as great as hers. As a result,
the officers inform the woman that she must acquire a restrain-
ing order if they are to arrest him in a future similar situation.*

The huddle in front of the apartment building is an explicit attempt by the officers to match the incident with the legal code to determine what legally permissible actions are available. They survey the situation comprehensively and measure it against possible legal infractions. The public-private distinction is of clear relevance in determining which behaviors are illegal and therefore grounds for arrest (about which more later). As it stands, however, they lack the necessary evidence of physical abuse. They thus inform the woman of the steps she must take to secure an arrest, and they leave the scene.

> A sergeant is driving one of several patrol cars that respond to a call concerning a possible burglary from the roof of a business. The primary A car responding calls for a helicopter, which quickly arrives. Its spotter discerns three young men on the roof, who flee when the helicopter arrives. The spotter is able to monitor the escape route of one of the suspects and radios that he is at the counter of a nearby hot dog stand. The sergeant arrives at the hot dog stand and notices a single customer. He searches the suspect, then pulls him out into the street so that the officer in the helicopter can identify him. Once he is identified, the suspect is returned to the building from which he ran. The other officers in the area continue to search for the other two suspects, to no avail.
>
> A young woman who made the initial call to the police is summoned to attempt to identify the captured suspect as one of the group she saw climbing onto the roof. She is unable to do so. Meanwhile, the helicopter officers survey the roof of the business and report that they discern no signs of forcible entry. The suspect has no identification, so the officers are unable to perform any checks for outstanding warrants. As a result, the officers have little recourse but to release him. This is an outcome that clearly disappoints many of the officers, who are convinced that a burglary was in progress and are upset because the suspect was clearly running from the police. They let the young

man go, but not without letting him know that he "got lucky this time."

Again, the inability of the police to demonstrate the occurrence of a crime limits their ability to respond to a situation that, upon casual inspection, seems to provide evidence of wrongdoing.[13] Although the initial reports and the flight of the suspect from the roof are enough to justify detaining and questioning the suspect, the lack of reliable eyewitness testimony and of physical evidence of an actual break-in means that the case cannot proceed further. In this instance, a lecture is the most punishment the officers can legally inflict.

A sergeant is summoned to a minimall by a patrol officer team. When he arrives, he discovers the two officers in conversation with a woman. The woman is holding a pamphlet from a local gay and lesbian resource center that discusses harassment based on sexuality. The woman is insisting that the officers file a report on a man she claims so harassed her. The officers are resisting her request and have summoned the sergeant to buttress their position. The incident, it turns out, began as a dispute over a parking spot in the mall's crowded lot. The man believed that the woman unfairly cut him off, which motivated a verbal outburst. During his harangue, he apparently referred to the woman as a "fat dyke bitch," which prompted her to call the police. The officers, however, insist that this does not fit the legal definition of the crime in question, primarily because the man does not know the woman and thus knows nothing of her sexual orientation. They also point out that the argument primarily concerned a parking spot, and thus was not an overt and premeditated attack on her sexual orientation. The sergeant agrees with the officers and patiently explains why neither an arrest nor a report is justifiable.

In this situation, the officers again measure the incident against their understanding of the law and base their actions on that understanding. Their interpretation here, however, is clearly arguable. The man did use an inflammatory term, which perhaps provided enough justification for a report. The officers' reluctance to proceed could thus be interpreted as their own, more subtle, version of homophobia, or as a simple desire to get on to other things. However, the officers do find the man inside one of the mall's stores, bring him out to the parking lot, explain the situation to him, and work calmly and patiently to override his initial objections to convince him to apologize to the woman. In other words, they do treat the situation and the woman's complaints seriously and go to some lengths to achieve a resolution. Thus, neither homophobia nor convenience seems to explain their reluctance to take a legalistic course. In any case, the law clearly works as a prism through which officers define the situation and determine a course of action.

These are just three incidents, but they illustrate the fact that no matter what extralegal considerations pertain, the police still consciously and regularly use legal prescriptions to define the nature of the situations they encounter. The law is thus an important ordering system for the police in deciding whether and how they should act, whether they should assert their authority to the point of force or withdraw from intervening in social life.

Defining Spaces

The law is also, relatedly, an important ordering system when officers socially construct the spaces they control. The work on police discretion demonstrates that understandings of geography affect how officers enforce the law. However, these geographic understandings are partially constructed in the first place *by* the law, because the crimes defined by law influence how officers view different areas. For example,

one of the principal means officers use to distinguish the
different Basic Car Areas is in terms of the crime they will
find there. In fact, they rate their interest in working each
area in terms of the type of criminal they like to capture.[14]
For instance, officers who enjoy engaging gang members
like to work A91 and A29. A91 includes the intersection of
Smiley and Hauser, the most infamous street corner in the
division (see Map 2). In a four-square-block area centered on
that corner, two gangs have a clear presence — a Latino gang
known as 18th Street and an African-American gang known
as the Geer Street Crips. Relations between the Geer Street
group and Wilshire officers are especially hostile because of
a history of shootings between the two groups. The area is
also known as a good location for officers seeking felony arrests;[15] many of the young men found on the street are often
wanted on outstanding warrants and thus represent fairly
easy arrests.

A29 is part of the territory of Mara Salvatruncha (MS), a
Salvadoran gang reputed to be ruthless and evasive. The gang
reportedly engages in drug sales and robberies. Working A29
is seen as especially challenging because of the activity MS
generates and because MS is both dangerous and, unlike the
Geer Streeters, uninterested in any contact with the police.
Thus, confrontations with MS are difficult to engender, which
poses a challenge to officers especially interested in gang crime.

Robberies and stolen cars dominate the crime pattern in
A47 and A87. Officers working these areas are likely to spend
a large amount of time paying close attention to cars for the
various signs of theft — broken locks, punched ignitions, license plates whose cleanliness does not match the cleanliness of the car. They will also spend much time entering license plate numbers in their mobile display terminals, in-car
computer terminals that allow them access to Department
of Motor Vehicles information. Officers can quickly learn

whether a car bearing a specific license plate has been reported stolen.

A75 is infamous among officers because of Washington Boulevard, long a home to prostitutes and drug dealing. Officers generally dislike working this area because prostitution is a difficult crime to detect[16] and because the area lacks much gang activity, save a small area across from the station known as the turf of the Schoolyard Crips. The other three areas of the division, A1, A33, and A61, are prized only because their crime pattern is minimal; officers who prefer to work less hard, or who enjoy "freelancing," like to work these areas. Call loads are often low, so officers can either relax or freelance throughout the division, traveling to help with the crimes in which they are most interested.[17]

By now it should be clear that the law, because it defines the various crimes the police are responsible for uncovering, is a principal component in structuring how the officers view the situations they encounter and the various areas in the division. By defining those actions that constitute crimes, the law also shapes whether the officers can or cannot legally proceed with various actions, such as arrest. But the permissibility of such actions is strongly conditioned by *where* events are occurring.

The Zoning of Permissible Action

Restrictions in Private Space

As the story concerning the domestic dispute illustrates, the range of permissible police actions is significantly determined by where an incident occurs. The officers were invited into the apartment but did not find the necessary evidence for an arrest. Their only possible arrest was for public drunkenness, but the man was in public space only because he followed the officers' orders. The distinction between public and private space is perhaps the most critical spatial delimitation that conditions police action.[18] The barriers that surround private space are often quite significant and are not always surmounted easily.

> *A woman calls the police and complains that her neighbor to the rear is throwing bottles over the fence and onto her drive-way. This is not only a nuisance but also a violation of a re-straining order. When the officers knock on the door of the al-leged offender's house, a friend answers. As she responds to their questions, she reaches for a folding chair, opens it, sets it squarely in front of the door, sits down, and continues to talk. Her ac-tion is unambiguous, a clear statement that she knows the police are not allowed to enter without her permission. Unable to enter and question the offender, the officers have little choice but to leave. They are not likely to take the next potential step, to se-cure a search warrant, given the comparatively unserious nature of the complaint.*

Here, the mundane act of sitting in a chair serves as a pow-erful territorial marking and quietly rebuffs police officers who have evidence of wrongdoing. This capacity of private space to shield citizens from the police works in this case to help a sus-pect elude capture. The distinction between public and pri-vate space is clearly recognized by all concerned, and the po-lice choose to retreat. Crossing the boundary requires a further legal action, securing a search warrant; the police must turn to a higher legal authority to gain permission to enter.

> *A senior lead officer is concerned about a house in which, she believes, several gang members are living and congregating. She is receiving complaints from the neighbors about loud par-ties during which random gunshots sometimes ring out. No one, however, actually has been seen shooting. What is worse, from the SLO's perspective, is that the owner of the house, an elderly woman who reputedly is one gang member's grandmother, is hos-*

tile to the police and refuses to participate in any attempts to restrain activities there. She refuses, in particular, to allow any officers on the premises. The SLO expresses frustration at her inability to place pressure on the residents within.[19]

Overcoming and Mobilizing the Private-Public Boundary

At times, the line between private and public space is clear and serves to limit the capacity of the police to intervene in some social situations. The permeability of the public-private boundary can vary situationally, however. If officers are tracing a series of clues from the fresh scene of a major crime or are pursuing a suspect fleeing from a crime scene, they can transgress private boundaries if necessary.

A worker at a small hamburger stand is held up at gunpoint. He complies with the robber's instructions to empty the cash register but is shot in the stomach anyway. An off-duty school district police officer sees the shooter escaping in a truck. The police follow a trail of clues to the apartment of the girlfriend of the registered owner of the truck. Although the woman resists police entreaties that she let them in, the officers assure her that they have the legal right to come in and that they will acquire keys to the apartment from the building manager if necessary. She ultimately relents. The officers enter the apartment, search it thoroughly, and detain all four people inside for questioning.

In some cases, police officers look to an outside authority to grant them the necessary permission to enter private space.

A woman known for prostitution wheels a paraplegic from a board and care home to her apartment and locks the door behind them. The attendants at the facility trace the man to this location but have no luck convincing the woman to unlock the door. The paraplegic is not unhappy about the situation, but his at-

tendants are concerned for his well-being. When the police ar-
rive, the sergeant in charge takes care to establish that the atten-
dants believe the man to be in a life-threatening situation. They
assure him that they do; not only is the woman unstable, they
point out, but the man admits that he is not presently in his
wheelchair, which makes him especially vulnerable. Further, the
woman is claiming to be armed with a knife. With the attendants'
concern thereby documented, the sergeant orders the door to be
kicked open. The woman puts up little resistance, and the man
is wheeled home.

A woman with a history of mental health problems has lost
legal custody of her daughter to her own mother. While her
mother is out shopping, the woman swipes the untended girl,
returns to her own apartment, and locks the door. The police
arrive and try to convince the woman to release the girl, but
she refuses. They radio in a request to the county agency that
placed the girl with her grandmother for permission to enter the
apartment. When the permission is granted, the police secure keys
to the apartment from the landlord. When they open the door,
the young girl bolts out and is returned to her grandmother.

As these incidents illustrate, the police can overcome the
private-public boundary when a fresh crime has occurred or
when other social agencies issue the appropriate permission.
If certain legal requirements are met, in other words, the
private-public boundary becomes more permeable.

Importantly, the boundary outlining private space is not
just a restriction on police action that may or may not be
situationally overcome. In some cases, police officers themselves seek to make the boundaries around private space more
trenchant and use transgression of the boundaries to their
advantage. Thus, the private-public boundary can be not just
a limitation, but also a resource the police can use to impose
order.

When the owner of a gas station seeks police assistance in preventing transients from loitering on the property and offering window-washing services to his customers, the responding officer's first step is to require the owner to post "No Trespassing" signs. Once they are posted, the officer begins to warn the transients regularly and sternly that the signs clearly empower him to cite and arrest them should they remain. The transients leave.

An officer responds to ongoing citizen complaints about drug dealing around an apartment building by first approaching the owner of the building. She secures both the keys to the apartment building and the owner's permission to arrest anyone found loitering in the hallways. She adopts this strategy because many of the young men alleged to be involved in the drug trade do not live in the building and thus may legitimately be arrested for trespassing. The officer begins a series of raids on the building, hoping arrests for trespassing will serve to stem the drug dealing.[20]

A group of homeless people is living in a small encampment on a vacant lot. After receiving complaints from the neighbors, an officer meets with the owner of the property and secures his promise to erect a chain-link fence around its perimeter. In the interim, the officer regularly visits the site and warns the men that they will be arrested if they remain after the fence goes up. When the fence is finished about a week later, the officer arrests two men, which convinces the others to leave. In this case, the fence is actually not legally necessary for the arrests to be justified. However, the officer wants the boundary around the property clearly marked so that the homeless men's transgression is visible to all concerned.

All three of these vignettes illustrate the clear use of territoriality as, in Sack's term, a "strategy" to influence the be-

havior of people who are seen as a threat to particular definitions of public order.[21] In these cases, the boundary between
public and private does not restrict the police, but rather enables them to create and enforce order. The officers work to
make the boundary as trenchant as possible, then enact the
boundary by clearing the area of unwanted activity. The legal demarcation between public and private is quite obviously of great significance here; paradoxically, officers who
in one instance express frustration at its existence will in another use it to achieve a particular goal.

Restrictions in Public Space

The distinction between public and private space is thus a
significant one for the police and serves as a primary means
to delimit the range of permissible actions available to police in establishing order.[22] Many analysts of the police have
pointed out that the public versus private space distinction
builds an implicit class bias into police patrol; because lower-
class, often minority, people spend more time in public space,
they receive more police attention.[23] The mere appearance
of individuals in public space does not mean that the police's legal capacity to act is unhindered, however. The police
do have the right to attempt to question citizens in public
space, but they do not always have the right to require the
citizens to respond. Without "probable cause" to believe that
a person has committed a crime, the police are not legally
allowed to impede a citizen's escape should the citizen not
wish to be detained. Thus, for example, an officer cannot pull
her car in front of a pedestrian she wishes to question, because such an action effectively detains the pedestrian.

The "probable cause" requirement for detention requires
considerable effort on the part of police who wish to investigate a potential suspect without overstepping this legal bound-

finding and legally detaining people who may be involved in criminal activity. For example, a group of young men dressed in gang attire cruising a middle-class street in a vehicle blaring loud rap music will undoubtedly attract the attention of a passing patrol car. At that point, the officers may be eager to detain the car: they may be convinced the young men are or will be involved in criminal activity, they may feel a need to protect the neighborhood from an unwanted incursion, or they may feel personally challenged by the appearance of a stereotypical rival. To detain the car, though, they need probable cause. The officers will thus search for evidence of vehicle code violations or of unlawful driving (exceeding the speed limit, excessively loud music) to enable a legal detention.

Creative use of probable cause can earn officers praise. For example, one patrol car team received a commendation for detaining a group of young men because of a vehicle code violation. One of the men had a conspicuous bulge at his waistband, which the officers used to justify a search of the men and the car. The search yielded two guns and four arrests. The officers were officially rewarded for using probable cause to secure the arrests.

This example of successful "pooping and snooping" illustrates how officers work with legal rules to investigate situations of concern to them. In other words, the boundary between public and private space is not necessarily fixed and permanent, but is open to redefinition in certain circumstances. Pooping and snooping, in fact, often requires that officers do what they can to loosen the restrictions that pertain to private space.

Further, the existence of legal restrictions on officer access does not mean that the police will abide by them. It may also be the case that citizens will feel intimidated by officers into agreeing to be detained even though they have the legal right to walk away.[24] Officers may even feel confident that they can construct a post hoc description of a scene such that they can convince a superior, a judge, or a jury that they felt a legitimate sense of danger and thus were compelled to detain or search a suspect. This was precisely the strategy the officers charged in the beating of Rodney King used to justify their massive use of force.[25]

On the other hand, two of those officers were eventually convicted and imprisoned, and their legal plight is often discussed by current LAPD officers.[26] In addition, a massive recent growth in successful civil lawsuits against LAPD officers also restricts their willingness to ignore legal restrictions. In just three years, from 1991 to 1993, more than $45 million was paid to people who filed suit against individual police officers and the department. LAPD officers still often ignore legal restrictions on their capacity to detain, search, and use force, but they increasingly recognize the potential damage such actions can cause to their careers.

Other Legal Considerations

The rules surrounding the public-private space distinction and those concerning probable cause thus strongly condition the spatial range and the nature of permissible police action. Other legal rules also restrict or otherwise regulate police territorial actions.

On a slow Saturday afternoon, a senior lead officer enters the watch commander's office seeking advice on a call he has just received from the parents of a sixteen-year-old girl. The parents say that the girl has left home and taken up residence in her boyfriend's apartment. The parents want the police to forcibly bring the girl home. The SLO's question is whether he can legally carry out this request. A long discussion and a consultation of the criminal code reveal that he can do so only under one stipulation: that the parents legally state that the girl is uncontrollable and that they therefore relinquish her to the dominion of a county agency. Veteran officers participating in the discussion say that this is a change from earlier times, when they would quickly, and legally, have acceded to the parents' request.

Thus, however much the officers feel saddened by the parents' plight and wish they could fulfill their request, legal definitions of parental rights restrict their capacity to act. In this case, legal regulations restrict their capacity to, in effect, carry out the parents' desire to enact a territorial strategy to reassert control over their daughter's behavior. In other situations, legal rules may *require* that the police enact particular territorial actions. For example, in cases of domestic violence, police officers in California are required to adopt the territorial measure of jailing any suspect when there is clear evidence of injury. Thus, if one of the combatants is sporting a bruise that is likely to have occurred during a recent incidence of violence, the likely perpetrator is immediately handcuffed and taken to jail, regardless of whether the victim wishes the arrest to occur. In most domestic violence cases, even without clear evidence of injury, common police practice is to separate the involved parties, to help restore calm and to make it easier for each side to describe the situation without challenge or intimidation from the other.

Concerns of Civil Liability

Domestic disputes thus place considerable police attention on required or recommended territorial actions. In these cases, arrest is required. In other situations, arrests may not occur because the law specifies that they must occur, but because officers are afraid of potential legal consequences should the arrest not occur. This is a component of a broader police fear of potential civil suits that may be lodged against them. An arrest can be seen as a means to ward off such a suit.

> *An ambulance driver requests police assistance because he is being threatened by a passer-by. When the officers arrive, they discover that the citizen in question is an inebriated transient who is now across the street and walking away from the ambulance. The officers drive over to the man and detain him for questioning. A computer check reveals that the man has outstanding arrest warrants totaling more than $2,000.[27] The man is clearly drunk, however, and does not appear to pose a threat to anyone. He maintains that his home is just two blocks away and that he will go there quietly if he is not arrested. The sergeant in charge chooses to arrest the man, not because of a violation of the law but because he fears that the man's inebriation might cause him to cross the path of an oncoming car; the sergeant is afraid of a civil lawsuit if he fails to protect the man from unnecessary harm. He instructs the patrol car officers to take the man to the station.*

It is not possible to outline here the full range of legal rules and regulations that structure police territoriality. To this point, however, the discussion has suggested that the law shapes how police officers conceptualize the areas they patrol by defining the crimes they are likely to encounter in those areas; the various spatial parameters that officers must take seriously; and the range of permissible and required territorial actions. It should be clear, therefore, that the law is a principal normative order in the structuring of police territoriality. It is also true that legal evidence of a crime does not always impel police action, nor does the lack of such evidence prevent it.

Ignoring and Enlarging the Law

A sergeant discovers a homeless man removing copper pipe from a construction site and loading it into a shopping cart. The construction site is clearly marked as private property and is bounded by a chain-link fence. The sergeant observes, though, that the fence is not well constructed and that the piping was placed next to the fence's edge. In other words, the thievery he witnessed was not a difficult job. The officer does compel the thief to return the piping, but he chooses not to arrest him because he places primary responsibility for the theft on the property owner's lax security.

In this situation, legal rules enable the officer to make an arrest, but he chooses not to because of what he perceives as a lack of "common sense" on the part of the property owner. A similar neglect of pure legal considerations explains why officers are reluctant to arrest the numerous street vendors who operate throughout the division. Their reluctance stems from two factors: the vendors' ubiquity, and the officers' sympathy for the vendors' initiative. As a result, arrests of street vendors are rare, and occur only as the result of a citizen complaint.

Legal stipulations alone are thus clearly not enough to ensure police action. In these cases, "common sense" and sympathy for hard-working people constrain the police from exercising their legal power to arrest. In the next five chapters I explore in more detail the variety of extralegal considerations that police often take into account in choosing how to act.

At the same time that legal grounds do not necessarily constitute a sufficient condition for an arrest, the lack of a clear or pressing crime does not necessarily eliminate an officer's capacity to use territoriality.

When an office worker at a local Jewish temple calls the police and complains about a transient who is maintaining a regular presence in the parking lot, the sergeant is unsure how to act. The transient is not an obvious nuisance—he is not harassing anybody, he is not urinating or defecating in public. Further, the man is Jewish, so the sergeant believes the temple should assume some responsibility for his care. Thus, the sergeant does not want to arrest the man. The office worker, however, would still like the man removed. The sergeant patiently asks the transient if he will allow himself to be transported to another area. The sergeant quietly but persistently continues to offer to give the man a ride elsewhere, and the man eventually accepts.

In other cases, officers are not so polite.

A senior lead officer on regular patrol on a Friday night is especially attuned to various groups of teenagers gathered on sidewalks and street corners. He has no legal means to arrest or detain any of these youths, but he is bothered by their presence. He stops whenever he sees such a group and declares, "There is no hanging out around here." He never threatens to arrest them, because he has no basis for doing so. He merely hopes that his ongoing presence and harassment will convince the teenagers to gather someplace else, preferably inside.

Such a strategy can be augmented by bluffs. Officers can take advantage of potential ignorance of the law to back up their requests for dispersal by suggesting that they can decide to make arrests.

An officer encounters a transient couple who are flagging down motorists at a stop sign and offering to wash their windows. The officer is responding to citizen complaints that the couple have become aggressive with motorists who refuse them. The officer arrives on the scene, pulls the couple to the sidewalk, and threatens to arrest them because of an ordinance that ary. Thus, officers who suspect that a car may be stolen look vigorously for evidence of failure to meet vehicle code specifications (burned-out lights, bald tires, etc.). Or the officers will merely tail the suspect car, hoping that a guilty party's anxiety will result in erratic driving that justifies a vehicle stop.

> *A senior lead officer is cruising through his area when he meets a car with a burned-out headlight coming from the other direction. The SLO immediately does a U-turn and follows the car to a driveway a block away, where it parks. The officer approaches the driver and uses the headlight infraction to justify a request to see his driver's license. The officer runs a check on the name, and the dispatcher returns with an indication that there may be an outstanding felony warrant for the driver. This prompts the officer to handcuff the driver and take him to the station.*
>
> *Further digging reveals that there is not in fact an outstanding warrant for the driver. He does, however, possess an impressive criminal record, most of which was compiled in the nearby city of Compton. Despite the fact that there is no warrant, the SLO is happy with the results. He had heard that this young man had recently moved into the neighborhood and was rumored to be trying to establish a drug operation. This possibility worries the SLO not only because he wishes to stem drug trafficking but also because he knows any move to establish a new dealer in the area will be met with violent resistance. The SLO is thus happy that he has been able to confirm that this young man does represent a potential threat to the neighborhood and is worth his continued attention. The broken headlight, which he characterizes as an "opening," enabled him to legally gather information on someone he considers a potential threat to the area.*

This ability to search for evidence of probable cause is central to the practice of "pooping and snooping," the art of *forbids window washing. The officer later admits that no such ordinance exists; the threat was a bluff to citizens who were not likely to be aware of the law.*

Conclusion

A full outline of the various legal parameters that structure police territoriality is not necessary to establish this chapter's central argument: that the law constitutes a normative order that conditions where and how the police can enact territorial strategies to secure public order. The law defines the principal boundary between public and private space, a boundary that police typically respect and that places clear limits on their mobility and power. On the other hand, the boundary can be mobilized by officers in their efforts to clear a place. Even within public space, however, the officers' capacity to circumscribe the movements of citizens is restricted. Without demonstrable probable cause, officers are not legally empowered to enact boundaries around the free movement of the citizens they encounter in public space. This demonstrates another of the chapter's central arguments: that the law not only bounds space in important ways for police officers, but also regulates the range of permissible territorial actions within those spaces.

The last section nonetheless makes plain that the law, while it is important, does not determine police action. This harks back to the discussion of police discretion cited at the outset of the chapter and provides a useful transition to subsequent chapters, which seek to elaborate five normative orders in addition to law that structure the practices of police territoriality. One of these normative orders is bureaucratic control, the subject of chapter 4.

4. THE BUREAUCRATIC ORDERING OF POLICE TERRITORIALITY

MODERN AMERICAN POLICING WAS TRANSFORMED by turn-of-the-century efforts to increase "professionalization" through effective bureaucratic control. Professionalization was a central component of the Progressive reform movements that attacked the corruption in many urban police departments.[1] Power was wrested from ward-level politicians and deposited in the hands of police chiefs who, via civil service protections, were made less vulnerable to shifts in the political winds. This faith in civil service regulations was part of a larger endorsement of scientific management, and this was seen as a way to increase police legitimacy.[2] The police were to be organized along clear, rationalized lines, with well-developed rules for promotion. To avoid the ad hoc decision making of boss-dependent policing, these more professional officers would be beholden instead to a well-regulated bureaucratic order administered by a powerful chief insulated from city politics.

This image was promoted heavily in Los Angeles, whose chief, William Parker (who served from 1949 to 1966), was a prominent national advocate of professionalized policing.[3] Parker succeeded in creating a police department whose practices and employees were largely protected from outside political intervention. He touted his department as a paragon of scientific efficiency and his officers as calm, fit, intelligent, and humorless.[4] No more obvious symbol of this new police officer existed than Joe Friday, the colorless "just the facts, ma'am" detective on *Dragnet,* a television show whose scripts were supervised by the LAPD.[5]

Parker's reform effort successfully insulated his department from outside political interference and increased internal control. A beefed-up Internal Affairs Division worked to ferret out any vestiges of corruption, and a rigorous boot-camp-style police academy sought to create a tough-minded officer filled with a strong sense of esprit de corps. Indeed, recruitment practices focused extensively on former members of the military, who were ostensibly well disciplined and accustomed to life in a hierarchical bureaucracy.[6]

As a result, the LAPD emerged as a national model because it had reputedly best developed a professionalized, bureaucratic order. There was of course an important downside to this new force: its detachment from the community made it less responsive than many political leaders wished to the ongoing complaints about racist uses of excessive force.[7] Nonetheless, the LAPD retained a strong sense of political autonomy for years after Parker's death, and it remained a national symbol of professional policing.

This apparent "success" at bureaucratization is challenged by a number of police researchers who have discovered a severe disjuncture between the stated bureaucratic goals of departments and their actual practices.[8] This disjuncture is largely understood as a function of the incompatibility between the rigidity of bureaucratic strictures and the shifting flux of events facing patrol officers. Most of the situations a police officer encounters cannot be anticipated, and thus cannot be effectively regulated; competent patrol requires a craft-like ability to adapt to the particular context of each incident,[9] an ability to be flexible and "situationally rational."[10] Patrol officers, aware of the need for flexibility and anxious to exercise their individual judgment, resist efforts to regulate their practices. They are able to resist because many of their supervisors, themselves former patrol officers, also appreciate officer initiative and thus control with a light hand. Supervision is limited anyway, because most patrol actions are not monitored. Further, a tight bonding between officers often works to shield mistakes from the awareness of supervisors.[11] Regardless, therefore, of elaborate bureaucratic rules and stringent efforts at internal control, police departments, like other organizations, sustain a significant gap between theory and practice.[12] Shielded from direct supervision and driven by a pride in their own competence, patrol officers are able to exercise considerable individual discretion in their daily practices.

It is important, however, to sustain the line of argument developed in chapter 3, that is, to pay proper analytic attention to legal and bureaucratic regulations. To say that such regulations do not control all police behavior does not mean that they have no effect. Just as legal rules condition where and how the police can act, bureaucratic regulations structure their territorial practices. The bureaucracy defines the parameters of territorial concern for each officer—the boundaries of the area for which he or she assumes responsibility. Bureaucratic rules also define the particular responsibilities the officer is to assume within that territory. Depending, in other words, on an officer's bureaucratically defined status, the range and nature of his or her territorial responsibilities varies significantly.

This chapter outlines the range of bureaucratically ordered territorial responsibilities and explains how functions vary across space as they vary across the organizational flowchart. These variances occur both horizontally and vertically within the organization. Horizontal variation refers to distinctions made across the organization between different units. In other words, responsibilities vary horizontally from one unit to another: from basic patrol to senior lead officers to narcotics to CRASH and so on. Responsibilities also vary vertically from one rank to another; as one climbs up the hierarchy, the nature and range of duties shifts. These various organizational positions define different ranges of territorial concerns and also the hypothetical points at which these concerns interlink and optimally interact. It is at these points of connection that considerable "slippage" occurs; rather than effectively coordinating complementary concerns, different units and different officers often work in (sometimes deliberate) ignorance of each other. The result is a reduction in police capacity to exert territorial control.

The goal of this chapter, then, is to develop an adequate understanding of the importance of bureaucratic structures to the practices of police territoriality. Such structures constitute a normative order because they define a set of rules and practices that are organized around a central value, in this case organizational control. The goal of these rules is to make the chain of command strong and individual responsibilities precise so that, at least ostensibly, control can be exerted over subordinates and the organization can effectively and unambiguously act in coordinated fashion to best secure public order. For an individual officer, the primary value at the heart of the normative order of bureaucratic control is professional self-preservation: officers learn that abiding by the rules means avoiding sanctions and advancing up the ranks. That these rules are inconsistent, sometimes contradictory, and often resisted or even ignored in regular police practice does not mean that they are impotent in structuring police territoriality.

Horizontal Variations in Territorial Concerns

Variations within the Wilshire Division

On regular patrol through his Basic Car Area, a senior lead officer observes a dozen Latino males on a street corner. The men are prospective day laborers, standing idly in hopes that someone will come by and hire them for short-term work. Although he is sympathetic to the economic plight of the men, the SLO has also received many complaints about them from residents of a nearby middle-class neighborhood. As a result, when he sees the men, he stops his car and orders them to disperse.

Two days later, a sergeant is on regular patrol. It is a slow day, so there is little to capture his attention. Nevertheless, as he passes the very same street corner and the same group of men, his response is to keep on driving. The presence of the men, even on a slow day, elicits no response.

These different responses to the same phenomenon result from the two officers' different sets of responsibilities. The senior lead officer, by dint of his bureaucratically defined duties, receives regular complaints from residents of the area for which he is responsible. The SLO is also officially urged to ignore radio calls, so that when he is on patrol he can respond to complaints. He expresses no satisfaction with this particular action — he understands the economic struggle of the day laborers — but his job is to reduce his complaints, and he is freed from the radio to monitor situations such as this one. As a result, he uses his coercive power to clear the area.

The sergeant's job, by contrast, is to supervise patrol officers. He monitors the radio and responds to calls that, in his
judgment, warrant a supervisory presence. He possesses the
same coercive powers as the SLO, and thus could roust the
men should he choose to do so. He does not, either because
he wants to remain free so that he can respond rapidly to an
emergency or because, unaware of the nearby residents' complaints, he does not consider the men to be a problem worth
his attention. Thus, although both officers drive through the
Wilshire Division in clearly marked police cars and possess
the same coercive power vis-à-vis the citizenry, they do not
respond to the same situation in the same manner; the particular zone of concern varies from car to car, as do the type
of territorial and other practices most likely to be exercised.

Officers in a Wilshire "A" car engaged in regular patrol,
for example, usually find themselves principally responding
to radio calls. In fact, on most occasions, A cars have a backlog of calls waiting in their "queue." As a result, only the
more flagrant criminal actions, or potential criminal actions,
attract their attention as they move from one call to the next.
As I mentioned in chapter 2, the spatial range of an A car
should be bounded by a Basic Car Area, but the heavy call
load means that each car spends much of each watch in other
areas.

As part of a "special problems" unit (or CRU), a "Z" car
will, by contrast, be attuned to a very specific crime in a very
specific area. Indeed, the effectiveness of the Z cars depends
in part on specifying the problem and the area as finely as
possible. SLOs also monitor a specific set of concerns, often
of a "public order" nature, which usually stem from citizen
complaints. SLOs can thus deal with day laborers or vagrants
ignored by patrol officers. SLOs can also pursue numerous
territorial strategies that can succeed only over a protracted
period of time. If, for example, a SLO is interested in stem-

ming the sale of drugs on a particular sidewalk, she can exhort the neighbors to provide ongoing surveillance to learn where the goods for sale are being stored. Or the SLO can put pressure on a landlord to evict tenants associated with drug sales. The SLO can even, in extreme cases, institute court procedures to deprive the landlord of ownership of a building if the landlord does not assist in stemming criminal activity.

Like SLOs, foot-beat officers are detached from the radio and concentrate on public-order concerns. Because foot-beat officers patrol in commercial areas, they particularly focus on homeless people, drunks, and street vendors, all of whom draw the ire of businesspeople. The foot-beat officers who patrol Wilshire Boulevard, for example, will urge homeless people to leave the boulevard but will ignore those they find one block north or south.

Extradivisional Operations

These four groups of officers—regular patrol, special problems, senior leads, and foot-beats—are all controlled from within the Wilshire Division and are monitored by supervisors there. Other units controlled by other branches of the bureaucracy also patrol the division. The gang unit, known as CRASH (Community Resources against Street Hoodlums), and the Narcotics Unit are both bureau-level enterprises. Their presence in the division is fairly regular, and they often get explicit invitations from senior lead officers. The SLOs, given their closeness to the community, are well aware of which areas are locations for either gang gatherings or drug sales, and thus will ask CRASH or Narcotics to "work" those areas. In the case of CRASH, working an area can mean staking out a particular location for several hours in hopes of detecting explicit signs of criminal activity. CRASH can also use its knowledge of particular gang members to its advantage. That can

mean arresting people the officers know have outstanding
warrants or exerting pressure on particular gang members
to "give up" the perpetrator of a recently committed crime.
Their intent is to "put the heat on" a gang to encourage its
members to take their activity elsewhere. CRASH thus marks
an area as one to which it will devote attention and from
which it will transport people to jail as part of a larger strategy to thwart the gang's efforts to control the area. This explains the senior lead's interest in inviting CRASH to pursue
its territorial actions; if the gangsters leave the SLO's area,
then the citizens of that area will be satisfied.

The identical motivation underlies SLO overtures to Narcotics. The principal means by which Narcotics works an
area is undercover buy-bust operations. In these operations,
an undercover officer approaches people on street corners
known for drug sales and elicits an offer from a potential seller.
At that point, officers who have been positioned on the four
streets surrounding the corner swoop in to arrest the puta-
tive seller. The intent is the same as that of the CRASH actions:
to clearly mark the corner as one where police intrusion —
which can result in jailings — can be expected. In effect, the
police and the dealers are engaged in a territorial battle; the
dealers hope that their potential customers clearly recognize
their corner as a place to come, while Narcotics hopes to
persuade the dealers to go elsewhere.

Another set of police actors, from the Metro Division, also
occasionally enters Wilshire. Metro consists of a number of
specialized units that are deployed, as the division's title
suggests, all over the LAPD's jurisdiction. These units include
the K-9 unit, SWAT (Special Weapons and Tactics), and the
Mounted Unit. Both K-9 and SWAT are called in to corral
dangerous suspects. In the case of SWAT, the suspect must be
armed and barricaded inside a building or apartment. The

Mounted Unit is brought in at an area captain's request to provide surveillance of a particular area; being on a horse provides an officer a wide range of sight and ease of maneuverability. In all cases, Metro officers must be explicitly requested, though, given other commitments, requests are not always granted.

Bureaucratic Tensions and the Failure of Territorial Control

The logic behind dispersing responsibilities across different bureaucratic units is obvious: if it is able to concentrate on a particular problem, a unit should be able to "solve" that problem most effectively. SLOs, as we have seen, are able to respond to public-order concerns in a way that patrol officers cannot, while CRASH is able to gather significant data on gang members and use that knowledge to monitor gang activity. The dispersal of duties across units is designed to increase the department's ability to secure control over the division's space.

In practice, however, this division of responsibilities can limit the capacity of the department to work efficiently. The strict division of responsibilities can mean that a given officer's awareness of a particular situation is limited, a problem exacerbated by the frequently poor level of communication between units. Communication between patrol officers and senior lead officers, for example, is a frequent source of tension and frustration for both sides. Patrol officers complain that SLOs do not keep them regularly apprised of the overall pattern of criminal activity in their area. Some officers on regular patrol act with a very limited knowledge base. They bounce from incident to incident and deal with each in ahistorical and ageographical isolation. This is especially true in a division, such as Wilshire, whose call load is high; officers ricochet from call to call, moving quickly from one part of the division to another.

SLOs, on the other hand, are not always aware of all that is occurring in their area, because they only get reports on crimes that are considered "repressible" — crimes that the police, through active patrol, can allegedly help prevent. The crimes that fall into this category include burglaries, robberies, and thefts. It is thus harder for senior leads to monitor, say, the pattern of gang activity in their area because they may not be receiving reports of gang crime. Thus, regular consultations with patrol officers could provide valuable information.

Failure in cross-unit communication also occurs along the organizational boundary between division and bureau units. Division officers regularly complain about the paucity of information regarding gangs and wish that CRASH officers regularly stopped by roll call. Narcotics officers, too, have little contact with division officers other than with senior leads, and even here the level of communication varies significantly from senior lead to senior lead.

The frustration of division officers with larger units is also illustrated by their complaints regarding the investigation of the shooting of an officer near Smiley and Hauser. The investigation was the responsibility of the Robbery and Homicide Division, a specialized detective unit that handles all officer-involved shootings. The unit is headquartered downtown, and its actions were not easily monitored by Wilshire officers anxious to see the shooters captured. Many officers interpreted the lack of visible RHD presence as a symbol of minimal interest in the case. This worried the officers because they believed that if the shooters were not captured, others at Smiley and Hauser would feel emboldened to act similarly.

Although the failure of communication across the various lines of the organizational structure can be attributed partly to the constraints of time and resources, part of the reluctance to share information probably stems from each unit's desire to ensure its bureaucratic survival.[13] In other words, officers in different units recognize that the justification for their bureaucratic existence depends upon their ability to commandeer exclusive control of a particular area of authority. Thus, a sergeant in CRASH touts his unit's specialized database as a reason to keep the unit centralized within the bureau rather than disperse it into its four divisions. Without centralization, he argues, the effectiveness of CRASH would diminish. On the other hand, the administrative standoffishness of CRASH, evidenced by its reluctance to attend roll call at patrol divisions, decreases the department's overall gang surveillance because it limits exchange of information. Patrol officers, in daily contact with gang areas, could update CRASH on recent developments and encounters. Similarly, CRASH could use patrol officers to monitor groups or people of immediate concern.

This sort of departmental fragmentation occasionally can be overcome through the creation of a "task force" to deal with a particular crime in a particular area. This is usually spearheaded by a senior lead, who attempts to coordinate the efforts of all available resources—patrol cars, special problems cars, Narcotics, CRASH, even the Mounted Unit—to keep a sustained eye on a particular area. However effective these forces may be, they require a tremendous effort to organize and sustain, and, as a result, they are quite rare.

At this point, it should be clear that territorial strategies are commonplace among a wide variety of LAPD officers and that a given officer's spatial range of concern and favored tactics vary from unit to unit. This division of responsibili-

ties, in theory, is designed to increase the department's overall capacity to exercise control, but in practice often works
to fragment units whose full effectiveness depends on coor-
dination with others.

Another important means by which officers are differenti-
ated is via the vertical ranking of status.

Vertical Variations in Territorial Concerns

One of the primary goals of the professionalization movement was to shore up internal authority. Reformers sought
to copy the military, with its clearly defined ranks and its
emphasis on the chain of command. This structure persists
in most police departments, and the LAPD is no exception.
There are not only different ranks — patrol officer, sergeant,
lieutenant, captain, and so on — but also often different classes
within each rank. An officer's rank is clearly displayed on
his or her uniform via stripes or bars. Thus, each member of
the organization knows at a glance where he or she stands
in the chain of command vis-à-vis any other member.

Owning the Scene

The chain of command is of particular interest in the present
context because it helps determine who "owns the scene" —
who has the ultimate authority at any site of police activity.
Struggles over effective ownership of crime scenes and tensions over the proper course of intervention represent some
of the most volatile points of contact between different officers and units. Much is at stake, especially if the situation is
ambiguous, dangerous, or unfolding quickly.[14] Questions of
how a given space is to be approached and secured are difficult ones, answered differently by different officers. The chain
of command is designed to alleviate confusion in these mo-

ments, and to enable the group to work cohesively. The fact that situations can be defined differently and that tactical decisions are disputable, however, means that control of the scene is often an object of struggle.

> *A sergeant heads out for patrol after briefly chatting with another sergeant, who is sitting in his car in the parking lot working on his patrol log. Shortly after leaving the station, the first sergeant responds to a call from an off-duty officer who is chasing someone who has thrown coins at his vehicle.*[15] *The off-duty officer has contacted a police dispatcher via his car phone. The sergeant on patrol radios the dispatcher that he is responding to the call. Shortly thereafter, however, the second sergeant, still sitting in his car in the parking lot, comes over the radio and states that an off-duty officer should not be in a chase, and that he should simply take the license plate number of the car and cease the pursuit. This angers the first sergeant, who believes that the scene became his when he radioed his intent to respond. The second sergeant is therefore overstepping his bounds. This particularly angers the first sergeant because his colleague is new to the division and thus cannot discern from the updates coming from the off-duty officer just how fast and dangerous the chase actually is. The first sergeant indicates that he will discuss the matter with his colleague when their paths next cross.*

> *Two patrol officers stop and question a group of youths sitting in a parked car. Two of the youths suddenly bolt from the car and run into a nearby house. The senior of the two officers immediately broadcasts a request for additional units to help capture the youths. A swarm of officers, including a sergeant, quickly arrives. The situation is confusing, and the senior of the two initial officers is trying to communicate over the radio where he would like to position each unit. For their part, the other officers are trying to get more information about the location and dangerousness of the suspects. The sergeant comes on the radio*

and suggests that the group switch to another radio frequency so that their conversation will not interfere with the ongoing flow of dispatch; the sergeant specifically suggests that they all go to the frequency known as Tac 8. The officer immediately responds, "Hold off on the 8" and continues to use the regular frequency. The officer thus both ignores a reasonable suggestion and publicly countermands a superior officer. As the initial responding officer, he is understood to have considerable say in how the situation is handled, but such power diminishes when a sergeant arrives. To publicly turn aside a sergeant's suggestion is a bold move, sure to be cited as evidence that the officer is insubordinate.[16]

Both of these scenarios illustrate how officers struggle to define "ownership" of incidents, how they skirmish to determine who will carry the authority to dictate tactics. A particular area of tension, as the second scenario suggests, frequently develops between patrol officers and sergeants. Officers are usually the first ones to arrive at a crime scene and are in charge until a superior officer arrives. The mere appearance of a supervisor may not be sufficient grounds for an officer to need to surrender control; in many cases the supervisor will take a passive stance to observe the officers at work. A sergeant who swoops in aggressively is disdained not only by patrol officers who wish to exercise their autonomy but also by other sergeants, who recognize the need for supervisors to be more detached. A sergeant is expected to resist the temptation to assume immediate control of a crime scene and should not, in most cases, be the first unit to respond to a crime. These actions, in the eyes of patrol officers, indicate a sergeant unwilling to allow the officers to exercise their authority to establish scenes for themselves and to develop their tactical capacity to control the spaces they patrol.[17]

The Struggle between Inside and Outside

The rank structure of the bureaucracy is designed to specify ownership of scenes, and often works to do so. It does not do so in all cases, however, nor does it do so to everyone's satisfaction. Much of this dissatisfaction stems from the existence of what Reuss-Ianni calls the "two cultures of policing"[18] — roughly speaking, "the troops" and "management." This split is also characterized as one between "outside" and "inside," between street cops and supervisors.

"Inside" cops are seen as extremely cautious, afraid of bold action not only for fear for their own safety but also for fear of disciplinary action. This explains their "by the book" orientation, their hewing as closely as possible to regulations in order not to attract negative attention to themselves.[19] In the case of supervisors, attracting little attention means not only being careful themselves but also trying to prevent their subordinate officers from overstepping their bounds. More careful supervisors caution their officers to stay in control and to document everything. In the post–Rodney King era, particular emphasis is placed on uses of force; many supervisors want patrol officers to use force discriminatingly and parsimoniously. In a roll call discussion of an officer-involved shooting in another division in which three officers shot a combined eighteen rounds, the watch commander stressed how, in the investigation sure to follow, "each shot must be accounted for." His message was clear: do not shoot unless you can provide a solid justification afterwards.

This cautious approach to patrol work angers the "troops." They express fear that the supervisors will not back them up if, in the heat or confusion of the moment, they act in a manner that later is found questionable. This fear stems not only from a desire to avoid bureaucratic sanctions but also from an implicit diminution of their authority and capacity to respond to situations as they see fit. Patrol officers generally prefer to respond to situations by their "instincts" and often prefer to take control of situations aggressively. Excessive worries about various bureaucratic stipulations prevent instinctual and aggressive action. Thus, patrol officers feel that their own initiative is blunted by excessively careful supervision and that their careers and daily safety can thereby be compromised. This is especially the case in the post–Rodney King era, when citizen complaints are being investigated more thoroughly and when officers' track records of complaints threaten to hinder their advancement. The officers thus see the command staff as caving in to community pressure for more adequate control of their actions, especially in terms of use of force.[20]

This is an inevitable consequence of what might be better termed not the post-King era, but the post-Parker era. The consequence of the fallout from the King beating—the hounding from office of Chief Daryl Gates, the establishment of not one but two independent commissions to investigate the LAPD, the passage of a city proposition that mandated departmental restructuring—is that the Los Angeles police are less shielded from the community. Parker successfully built a political wall around the department that his successors more or less maintained despite regular attacks. The removal of Gates and his replacement by Willie Williams, an avowed proponent of "community policing," represent a strong shift in the department's ideological orientation toward the public. One consequence of this shift is a more aggressive investigation of citizen complaints, which patrol officers deeply resent. No longer adequately shielded from public intervention, the officers claim that they are being sacrificed to the public by a command staff mostly interested in its own political survival.[21] Command staff members try to explain the new political reality facing the LAPD, but patrol officers retain a strong sense that they have been abandoned.

Feeling Abandoned

A patrol officer evokes the ire of an elementary school principal when he responds to a 911 call to the school's playground. The officer rushes to the scene and tries to discern quickly the nature of the problem (apparently a fight). The principal is also interested in "owning the scene," and thus the two clash. The officer's manner irritates the principal enough that she calls the area captain to complain. Given the principal's stature in the community, the captain dispatches a sergeant to make amends, a strategy that is successful. Later in the shift, the sergeant and the patrol officer cross paths. The officer maintains that he handled the situation well and that he thinks the captain should send the principal a letter telling her to "leave us alone." The sergeant laughs and says, "You know that's never going to happen."

Both officer and sergeant express frustration with an incident that illustrates how political considerations can prevent their commanders from protecting them when their authority to command space is, from their perspective, needlessly questioned. The officers in effect feel abandoned by their commanders. We will understand this sense of abandonment more clearly after a discussion of the other normative orders. In short, however, patrol officers view an excessively cautious and aggressively second-guessing command staff as eroding their capacities to act assertively, safely, and competently.

A sergeant recounts a recent incident to which one of his officers had responded. The officer apparently stopped a car because the driver was not wearing a seat belt. The officer intended only to issue a warning, but chose to write a ticket when the driver unleashed a string of racial epithets. The patrol captain, in reading the report, had suggested that rather than writing the ticket, the officer might have been better served by letting the man go. If the driver was looking for a fight, according to this logic, perhaps it was best not to engage him. This angers the sergeant because of what he terms the implicit message—that citizens can challenge the police with no risk of impunity. He thinks such a message threatens his authority and his safety.

A cautious command staff is disdained by the "troops" also because it erodes the officers' capacity to, in the words of one sergeant, "do the right thing," which may or may not, in his eyes, cohere with doing things "by the book." Doing the right thing in this context means being "situationally rational," responding to an incident on its unique terms and exercising the initiative inherent in what this sergeant would undoubtedly understand as the craft of police work.

Conclusion

This chapter illustrates how the horizontal and vertical structuring of responsibilities within the bureaucratic order of the LAPD shapes the spatial scope of officer concern and the range of relevant territorial practices, and describes some of the tensions along points of contact between different units and officers. The bureaucratic structure significantly determines where officers will be deployed and what will occupy their attention there. This delimitation of responsibilities also carries implicit and explicit expectations about the type of territorial practices the officers will engage. In the exercise of their responsibilities, however, different officers and different units conflict as each attempts to secure control of a scene and to establish organizational status. These tensions are not just bureaucratic in scope; they often reflect the workings of other normative orders and the incompatibility of these orders with more formal bureaucratic strictures. One of a group of less formalistic normative orders revolves around the values of adventure and manliness. This is the subject of chapter 5.

5. ADVENTURE/ MACHISMO AND THE ATTEMPTED CONQUEST OF SPACE

THE TWO PRECEDING CHAPTERS HAVE implicitly adopted a neo-Weberian emphasis on the more legalized and formalized operations of the police and attempted to trace their effects on police practices of territorial control. An excessive focus on structural procedures, however, can obscure a fuller understanding of the practices of a state agency such as the police because a number of less formalized but no less significant impulses also structure such practices as police territoriality. In other words, normative orders other than the law and bureaucratic control condition how the police make and mark space.

These orders are created and reinforced within the subculture of the police.[1] Although these orders draw upon values such as machismo and morality that are prevalent in the larger culture, they are given particular definition within the more limited world of patrol. One of these normative orders is adventure/machismo, a subcultural collection of rules and practices that values the courage, power, and aggressiveness of an officer eager to be pitted against the most lethal criminal enemies.[2] Unafraid to face dangerous challenges, capable even of handling themselves strategically in the face of potential death, such officers are rewarded with tremendous respect from others. An adventurous/masculine officer relishes the thrill of a pursuit, actively seeks out felonious criminals, and values the use of "instinct" (as opposed to bureaucratic regulations) as a guide to behavior. The capacity to throw one self into harm's way and to emerge unscathed and victorious can elevate one quickly in the status hierarchy of this normative order.

Conversely, one can be described as a "station queen," one of the more derogatory terms police officers use to label each other. The term refers to an officer who would rather be "inside" than "outside," someone who would rather attend to the safe predictability of paperwork than to the more variable and dangerous reality of patrol. The function of the word *station* in the label is obvious: it connotes the refuge of the inside. The word *queen* is equally clear; it is an unalloyed attempt to denigrate those who are less bold as effeminate. By implication, an officer who welcomes the potentially lethal challenges of patrol is not only valued, but valued as masculine. Conversely, the terms "real man" and "real cop" are frequently used to describe particularly courageous officers. The opposing terms "station queen" and "real man" and their frequent use within police ranks succinctly illustrate the importance of the normative order of adventure/machismo.

Machismo and the LAPD

The masculinist aggressiveness of the LAPD has long distinguished it among American police departments.[3] This aggressiveness has manifested itself in frequent recourse to force, large numbers of felony arrests, and random stops and searches of potential suspects.[4] Such tactics are widely reputed to be especially pronounced in minority areas.[5] The image of the Los Angeles Police Department as an agency designed to protect white citizens from the influx of dark-skinned immigrants was avidly embraced by Chief Parker during the 1950s and 1960s. Parker regularly lambasted civil rights groups for allegedly fertilizing anarchy and communism, and he explicitly exhorted white citizens to support a police department able to contain minorities territorially. In 1965, he said to a television interviewer, "It's estimated that by 1970, 45 percent of the metropolitan area of Los Angeles will be Negro. If you want any protection for your home and family, you're going to have to get in and support a strong police department. If you don't do that, come 1970, God help you!"[6] It is not surprising that Otis Chandler, owner of the *Los Angeles Times,* once described Parker as the "white community's savior, their symbol of security."[7] Parker's ideology undoubtedly resonated with many white Angelenos, long practiced in the arts of residential seclusion from minority communities.[8] It was a philosophy apparently shared by one of his successors, Daryl Gates, chief from 1979 to 1992, who made a series of telling verbal missteps that betrayed a racial bias.

Gates did little to counteract a continuing culture of machismo within the LAPD. Indeed, he embraced it with his development of the SWAT unit, a miniature Marine Corps within the police department, and with the purchase of ever more sophisticated helicopters and even a battering ram. Thus, by the time the Christopher Commission probed the LAPD's treatment of uses of force following the beating of Rodney King in 1991, it found that aggressive officers were almost never censured meaningfully. It should come as little surprise, therefore, that the normative order of adventure/

machismo continues to shape the practices of LAPD officers, and that it is most frequently invoked in minority-dominated neighborhoods.

This chapter spells out the significance of this normative order and describes how it conditions the ways in which officers construct and attempt to control the areas they patrol. In the first section I discuss the normative order and the ideal characteristics it suggests each officer should possess: courage, strength, aggressiveness, imperviousness to pain and death. The second section reveals the implications of this normative order for the practices of police patrol by spelling out the ways in which the adventure/machismo norm shapes how officers define and approach various areas and the types of territorial practices they are likely to use. The third section takes a more critical view of this normative order. In it I discuss the ways in which an emphasis on adventurousness and masculinity limits the utility of officers in a number of settings and potentially threatens the safety of officers and citizens. This order sits uncomfortably within a police organization striving to adopt the practices of community policing and thus produces numerous political tensions within the department.

The Normative Order of Adventure/Machismo

The senior lead officer is checking on a few "problem locations" in her area on a relatively peaceful weekday morning. She is interested in monitoring an apartment building where she is attempting to wipe out gang graffiti, and also an alleyway where stolen cars are being deposited. En route, however, she hears an undercover detective's radio report of gunplay at a gang member's funeral in the southern end of the division. The senior lead decides to respond, even though she is not officially compelled to respond to radio calls. Nor is the incident occurring in her area.

Within two blocks of the scene, the officer, heading south, is stopped at a red light. Suddenly, a westbound car speeds in

*front of her. The officer hesitates, but cannot resist; she turns
right and gives chase. Her hesitation, however, has cost her. She
is too far behind the car and is barely able to see it turn north
on a side street. Once she reaches the side street and also turns
north, the car is gone. She mutters her disappointment.*

*The scene of the alleged gang fight also disappoints her. A
single man has suffered a small stab wound from what was actually a dispute over some groceries. No gang members, it turns
out, were involved; it was simply a comparatively minor incident on a sidewalk that the detective happened to see as he followed the gang funeral.*

The scenario, despite its ultimate lack of action, illustrates
the pull of adventure that many officers feel. In this case, an
officer felt compelled not only to be part of an attempt to
confront gang members but also to chase a speeding car
that she suspected was somehow involved. Despite concerns
about safety, especially with a ride-along in tow, the officer
responded to a potentially dangerous call and gave chase at
high speeds. And she expressed clear discontent when the
chase proved fruitless and the "gang crime" uninteresting.
The potential challenges and thrills of facing the most dangerous and implacable police foe, the violent gang member,
and of chasing a group of gang members in a high-speed pursuit, are highly valued by the adventure-seeking cop. Such
encounters enable officers to test their courage and their instincts against the unpredictable and potentially deadly actions of their most resolute opponents.

The thrill of pursuit is a central aspect of the adventurous
officer's professional identity. Pursuit provides danger and
demands instant reactions. Pursuits also provide the potential for a capture, for a clear police victory; the one who attempts to elude the police becomes an immediate foe, with
interests directly opposed to the officers'. To secure space well
enough to "corral the mustang" means an assertion of con-

trol over those who resist police authority. Thus, at the end of a pursuit, officers are wont to discuss the chase with others, to relive the length and the danger of the chase, to glory in the successful conclusion of a suspect in handcuffs.

An officer who is willing to plunge into pursuits, to aggressively "buy" "hotshots,"[9] is referred to as a "hardcharger" — unafraid to push relentlessly into potential peril. Such an officer displays the sort of courage heralded by the department's highest honor, the Medal of Valor, which commonly is awarded to those who endanger their own lives to rescue a citizen. Hardchargers overcome their own fears and put themselves in situations that are potentially fatal.

Indeed, a certain imperviousness to death seems an entrenched part of police subculture. Officers can be almost jovial about it.

Laughing at Death

I am on my sixth ride-along with a sergeant with whom I have developed a strong rapport. On patrol on a Friday night, the sergeant is requested to come to an apartment building. When we arrive, we learn that a young man has committed suicide by shooting himself in the head. The sergeant does not ask me whether I want to enter the apartment but rather says, "C'mon, Steve." It seems, in other words, particularly important to him that I enter the apartment with him to see the scene. I do so.

The apartment, which the young man shared with his mother and brother, is cramped and stuffy. The young man is on the kitchen floor, a pool of blood under his head, a high-powered rifle at his side. The sergeant begins to examine the rifle and the bullet wound. The scene is too much for me; overcome with sadness and stifled inside the apartment, I retreat. Outside, I become aware of the young man's mother, who is hysterical and unresponsive to her other son's attempts to comfort her. My sadness only increases, and I happily accede to the request of another sergeant's ride-along to escort her to a restaurant across the street so she can use the bathroom.

When we come back across the street and return to the scene, we discover the two sergeants laughing about my reactions. There are comments about the quickness with which I left and the apparent paleness of my face. The moral of their laughter seems clear: I do not have the requisite toughness to handle police work. For my part, I am struck that neither officer seems particularly affected by the sadness of the situation, by the ongoing wails of the bereaved mother, by the despair that must have preceded the suicide.

On another evening, a sergeant is requested at the scene of a shooting. Apparently, a young man had driven through an intersection wearing the wrong color baseball cap. The cap was blue, and the neighborhood is the territory of the Rolling 20's, a Blood gang. Two members of the 20's, standing on the sidewalk, saw the blue-capped man sitting in his car at a traffic light and shot at him. One of the bullets passed through the man's baseball cap, but only grazed the top of his head. Although he is alert and apparently fine, the victim is taken to a hospital by paramedics. The various officers who respond to the call find great amusement in examining the baseball cap, laughing at how close a call it represents. They show it off to all newly arriving officers and to curious spectators.

Each of these scenarios illustrates the attempt to make death and the potential for death laughable. This may mostly serve as a coping mechanism to minimize the ever-present fear of death that must lie underneath the surface of police consciousness. In effect, laughing at death seems to make it more controllable, to make the officers strong and self-reliant again in the face of their all too obvious mortality. To place oneself in the path of death, which the adventurous cop must do, is to need to develop a certain detachment from it, and detachment makes laughter possible.

Gunfighters

Of course, one way to conquer death, in this sense, is to become deeply familiar with the capacity to cause it. For this reason, perhaps, many officers become gun enthusiasts, not only striving to become proficient in their use but also intimately aware of various makes and models. The value of being able to use a gun well is obvious to all police officers; the capacity to shoot accurately under pressure can equal the capacity to save their own lives or the lives of others. Officers who qualify wear medals that attest to their "sharpshooter" status. The more adventurous and aggressive officers often appear to go a step further and develop a fondness for and knowledge of guns that extends beyond mere proficiency in use. Such officers are constantly exchanging information about guns they have purchased and their capacities, about which guns are useful to carry as additional backup, about types of guns used by criminals in calls they have handled recently.

In some cases, however, officers are acknowledged to be perhaps too anxious to use guns or to demonstrate their general prowess by flashing their weapons. Such officers may retrieve their shotguns from the rack inside the car on calls that other officers do not think warrant shotguns. They may be slow to return a shotgun to the car when the call turns out not to be dangerous. One officer glared when a sergeant told him to return his shotgun to his car on a call that was initially described as a bank robbery but turned out to be a minor gang altercation. The sergeant explained that the officer considers himself a "gunfighter" and thus enjoys brandishing his weapon in public. The sergeant, however, recognizes that the public might be disturbed to see the shotgun, and ordered the officer to return it to the car.

The "gunfighter" term is occasionally used by police officers to describe a typically young officer unafraid to brandish or use a weapon as part of a hard-charging patrol style. Such an officer is sometimes said to be suffering from the "John Wayne syndrome," or is called an "Eastwood," the terms referring to prototypically tough, masculine, and violence-prone icons.[10] Many hard-charging, adventurous officers do not embrace weaponry in a particularly pronounced fashion, but several do.

This embrace of aggressiveness and of weaponry is in part a component of the often-militaristic approach of the LAPD. In this context, police officers construct themselves as the "cavalry," called to do battle with the opposing forces of gangsters and other criminals. Officers tell each other that they are "going in" when they approach a group of gang members during a sweep of Smiley and Hauser; a sergeant describes himself as a "paid mercenary" of the citizens of Los Angeles, there to control and capture the "enemy." Officers worry about clustering too many patrol cars at the beginning of a watch because it is reminiscent of Pearl Harbor, where unsuspecting naval vessels were summarily wiped out by the Japanese. Gang members are described as "terrorists."

Embracing military terms places the LAPD in a particular sort of relationship with both criminals and their victims, a point I develop in more detail in the third section of this chapter. For now, the principal emphasis is on how this language resonates with the normative order of adventure/machismo. Just as if they were members of the military (as many of them once were), the officers embrace the ideals of courage in the face of danger, of superior strength and firepower in the face of the irrational "terrorist" enemy. Comfortable with death and its means, eager to test their mettle against a foe, hopeful of bragging of their exploits and successes to their peers, adventurous and masculine cops charge hard into pursuits and other unpredictable situations. In other words, they seek out particular types of action and engage in particular types of territorial strategies to demonstrate their strength.

Machismo and the Structuring of Police Territoriality

The discussion of pursuits suggests the type of practices adventurous officers enjoy—those that involve a chase, a challenge, and, they hope, a capture. These officers seek out activities that provide a rush of adrenaline; they like "running with the hunters" and "hooking and booking" (handcuffing and jailing). Many of them prefer to concentrate their efforts on high-crime areas, where such challenges can more easily be engaged, where the "enemy" is more easily found. They particularly enjoy working A91 and A29, where gang members gather. Gang members present the most significant challenge. They are resolutely anti-police, and they embrace the very sorts of challenges many officers do; gang members, too, embrace the destructive power of the gun and the thrill of danger.[11] Just like the police, gang members seek the respect of others through acts of daring, courage, and physical prowess.[12] Further, both groups are interested in securing control over public space. As a result, confrontations with gang members present police officers with a direct challenge and an opportunity to prove themselves. In front of gang members, as one officer puts it, "You can't let them see you slip." According to another, gang members are sensitive to officers who seem careless or scared and will attack those points of weakness. It is therefore important to exude confidence and a sense of control on patrol at, say, Smiley and Hauser. On patrol in a gang area, an officer has a chance to demon-

strate the courage and strength so central to the adventure/
machismo normative order.

Officers sometimes seem to seek out antagonism from gang
members intentionally. On a slow night, a sergeant cruises
through the Smiley and Hauser area. His car window is up,
but he shines his flashlight on various people gathered on
the sidewalks. When his light lands on one African-American youth who doesn't appear to appreciate the attention,
the sergeant says, mostly to himself, "Do you love me?" On
another night, another sergeant is patrolling the same area.
He cruises down Smiley, monitoring the apartment buildings
his colleagues consider most dangerous. One pass through
does not seem to cause much of a stir from the young men
gathered on the street, so he retraces his path in hopes of so-
liciting some hostile glares.

Adventurous officers also enjoy working A47 and A87,
the two areas known for car thefts. The thrill here is not
just using sufficient sleuthing skills to detect a stolen car but
also the subsequent challenge of detaining the driver. Such a
situation is ripe with the potential of a pursuit, which provides the excitement of trying to enact territoriality in dangerous and challenging circumstances. Even if the pursuit
does not occur, the clear potential for one delivers a notice-
able punch of adrenaline.

Tactics

Adventurous/masculine cops, as this discussion suggests, tend
to view space in terms of the quarry they can capture and
the techniques they must employ to do so. They seek out locations where their search and capture abilities are likely to
be tested, where their capacity to remain in control while under pressure can be challenged. Space thus tends to be trun-
cated, to be thought of in terms of where the suspect is lo-

cated and how he or she can best be captured through the most artful positioning of personnel. This is the space of *tactics,* a fairly empty space composed of quarry and conquerors, a space organized along the grids and axes used to locate and control, to isolate and surround. This space is not understood as the space of homes and residences, where people live and feel a sense of attachment.

> *The officers in the helicopter respond to a call about a possible burglary in a South Central neighborhood. They are given a location and a description of a suspect. The pilot steers the helicopter to the area while the observer prepares to activate his FLIR (forward-looking infrared device), which registers heat-bearing substances in a glowing white. Before the FLIR is activated, however, a motion-sensitive light flashes on in an alleyway. His suspicions alerted, the observer trains his "nightsun" spotlight on a middle-aged man who is moving slowly through the alley with the assistance of a cane. The observer broadcasts the location of his newly discovered suspect to a patrol officer, who promises to respond. In the meantime, the observer continues to illuminate the man as he moves slowly out of the alley and down a street. The spotlight does not seem to affect the man in any way; he does not look up or alter his movements. In other words, he displays neither fright nor guilt. The patrol car arrives, and the officers order the man to put his hands behind his head and kneel in the street so he can be handcuffed. As the helicopter pulls off, the observer mutters, "Well, he sorta matched the description."*

The helicopter observer can defend his decision to illuminate a man who was in an alleyway in the vicinity of a possible burglary, but his parting comment reflects his own doubt that the man is indeed a plausible suspect. The observer seems little concerned about the experience of the man whose walk down the street became the object of such powerful attention; the lived experience of a walk in the night is of no real consequence to a helicopter officer concerned with the tactics of discovery and capture.

Similarly, officers who are posted on the perimeter surrounding a contained suspect and must keep residents from crossing into the area often refuse to explain to citizens what is occurring. The message is clear: the space is under police control and residents need not be involved in the activity taking place there. The police have utilized their capacity to tactically enact a boundary and thus have defined the space solely in terms of their practices, nòt in terms of the lived experience of its residents. To embrace the tactical techniques of space control can mean a significantly decreased awareness of other experiences of space.

> *The lieutenant is describing the new "unusual occurrence" training the department officers are undergoing in the wake of the uprising in Los Angeles in 1992 and how enjoyable it was to be part of the two-day seminar. What was especially exciting, he says, is that his group actually got to practice immediately what they had learned when the police were summoned to the UCLA campus because a group of Latino students was demonstrating at the faculty center. He describes the "rush of going code 3"*[13] *through Westwood, of mobilizing and marching onto campus, of seeing the exercise "work": the "problem people" were arrested, and the demonstration was dispersed. His conversation reveals no awareness of the content of the demonstration nor of the effect on the UCLA community of a strong show of police force; it was a tactical exercise, and a successful one.*

At times, the opportunity to engage in tactical exercises seems more important than the apparent goal of capturing a suspect.

> *A request comes over the radio for a Wilshire supervisor at an apartment building. Two supervisors show up and discover two patrol units from the contiguous Rampart Division that*

had initially responded to the call. A Volkswagen had appar-
ently driven past the building and someone inside the car had
shot at a group of young men gathered in front. The group on
the sidewalk had returned fire and then run to the back of the
building. A resident of the area says that some of the group
may have run into the parking garage beneath the building.
The Rampart officers want to tactically "sweep" through the
garage to make sure it is clear.

As the group is mapping its strategy, an officer who has been
posted at the rear of the building emerges to say that he has been
told that the young men scaled a fence and are gone. This pos-
sibility seems to make more sense than the report that the group
is hiding out in the parking garage. Nonetheless, the sweep goes
on. Five officers enter the garage with guns drawn and move
stealthily from support post to support post, from car to car,
maximizing the potential for cover while they check for signs
of the suspects. This takes several minutes and yields nothing.

In this scenario, the desire to sweep the garage seems to
outweigh evidence that suggests that the action is unnecessary. The chance to experience the adrenaline of moving, with
guns drawn, through a potentially dangerous situation is impossible to resist. In this case, it seems that the garage is defined as a danger largely to justify the tactics the officers want
to employ.

A Friday-afternoon event at a roller rink within a quarter mile
of the Wilshire Station draws about four hundred mostly Latino
youth. Their presence draws the attention of some African-
American youths, who drive by and fire weapons, although not
into the group. The police decide to close the event at the roller
rink and to disperse the group when it empties into the parking
lot. To do so, the sergeant in charge amasses all available offi-
cers, a group of about twenty, and orders them to don their riot
helmets. The group is split into two, and each fans out into a
line. Each officer carries a baton across the chest to exert pres-

sure against any who resist. The two lines of officers work from different angles to sweep the group into the street and away from the roller rink. At no time during this procedure do any of the youths display any hostility toward the police; far from threatening the police physically, the youths never even engage them verbally.

Given the lack of a palpable threat from the teenagers, the officers' mobilization seems overstated. It is questionable whether the dispersal is even necessary. Why not allow the event to continue and merely post a patrol unit in the parking lot to dissuade outside interference? Or, if dispersal is deemed necessary, why not use a few patrol cars to sweep through the area, a strategy that might have worked less quickly but could have been just as effective? This would have the advantage of keeping most patrol units in the field and responding to a growing backload of radio calls. It seems clear, in other words, that the officers in charge were prone to define the situation as dangerous and to deploy maximal resources to disperse the crowd.[14] The desire of the young people to define the roller rink in recreational terms is trumped by the officers' definition of the space as dangerous and in need of tactical emptying.

This discussion of how space gets defined by officers interested in demonstrating their prowess through dangerous and adventurous tactics suggests some of the potential problems with this normative order.

A Critical View of Adventure/Machismo

Officers anxious to prove their mettle via a strong and tactically smart response to a hot shot may well save the life of a citizen or fellow officer. The capacity to respond successfully to a dangerous situation is clearly an inherent part of the police role and a service the citizenry of Los Angeles expects the police to provide; dialing 911 is an act of faith that the police will respond speedily and effectively. A police force that strongly defines its goals and practices in terms of adventure/machismo, however, can end up needlessly denigrating other central aspects of the police function and can harm relations with the community.

An officer interested in responding to hotshots can easily neglect various other aspects of the police role. In domestic disputes, for example, the skills necessary for securing control of the space in question involve not courage and strength, but patience and compassion. In many disputes, it may not be clear exactly who the "bad guy" is; situations are often ambiguous and difficult to untangle. Officers who like a clear distinction between "good" and "bad" and want a culprit easily identified for capture are thus often frustrated by the inherent complexity of interpersonal disputes. In such situations, the craft of peacekeeping is the route to resolution, but the significance of this craft is implicitly disparaged by a focus on adventure: peacekeeping is "chickenshit," it is "social work," and therefore is not of interest.[15]

Women officers are often seen as possessing the patience and compassion necessary for handling disputes. For this reason, the Christopher Commission, which undertook a thorough if somewhat hurried review of uses of force by the LAPD, encouraged the continued recruitment of women into its ranks.[16] The commission, however, discerned a strong bias within the ranks against women officers, a bias clearly reflected in many of my conversations with officers. The bias against women is couched in the very terms of the adventure/machismo normative order: women do not possess the necessary strength and tenacity to do combat with the violent enemies of the police. As a result, according to this line of logic, a woman's fellow officers are endangered because she is unable to protect them.[17] Further, officers argue that the physical training exercises at the police academy have been made significantly easier to allow women to pass. This means that officers are physically weaker, and that they have not enjoyed the esprit de corps that emerges from the collective experience of undergoing strenuous physical challenges. Needless to say, such officers spend little time discussing the potential merits of less physically oriented police work outlined by the Christopher Commission and others.

An embrace of adventure means an implicit disparaging of the more traditionally feminine skills of managing interpersonal disputes and runs counter to some of the larger aims of "community policing," the latest reform movement sweeping the police profession. In the post–Rodney King context of Willie Williams's tenure as chief, community policing is seen as a means of repairing the extremely damaged public image of the department, particularly in areas heavily populated by racial minorities. Community policing can mean many things but essentially represents an attempt to increase communication between the police and the residents of the communities to which they are assigned.[18] It is a deliberate step away from the professional model of policing so adamantly championed by Parker and his successors, a model that advocated a strong separation between the police and the potential corrupting influence of community politics. It is also a step away from the militarism implicit in much professionalization, the aggressive tactics that often antagonize communities. Community policing advocates encourage demolition of the walls between the police and neighborhoods, and the forging of cooperative relationships between the two.

Police officers wedded to the adventurousness of the job are not especially receptive to community policing. They are not interested in community meetings, and they are not interested in the "order maintenance" tasks communities often express the strongest interest in seeing the police handle:

wiping out graffiti, rousting homeless people, and so on.[19] Community policing means projects, not hotshots; politics, not "police work." It is therefore disparaged by the officers who want to chase and jail the "bad guys" who plague the city. According to this line of logic, the public is better off leaving the job of policing to the experts, who will act to ensure, as only they can, that the public lives in peace.

This tension between the embrace of community policing and the desire of police officers to continue to be part of a tough, "ass-kicking" department underlies much of the current dissatisfaction of the "troops" with management that I discussed in the previous chapter. Adventurous cops want to be free from the mundane aspects of many radio calls (petty business disputes, complaints about loud parties) and from excessive management oversight so that they can control space in an unrestrained, instinctual fashion. These desires seem only more restrained under community policing, given its explicit mandate that officers respond more sensitively and regularly to citizen concerns. That management has sold out to "politics" in its embrace of community policing only means, for adventurous cops, further restrictions on their ability to do their version of policing. For example, on a call regarding a man brandishing a gun, the responding units end up reminiscing fondly about the "old days." By the time they arrive, no guns are visible. In the "old days," the officers suggest, they would have stormed into the house, cuffed everyone inside, and intimidated people into giving up the gun(s). As it stands, they end up merely issuing a warning to those gathered outside.

In following the Christopher Commission recommendations to investigate uses of force more aggressively, the department's managers are clearly attempting to restrain the excesses of adventurous cops. Many such cops are reputed to have engaged in precisely the practices employed against Rod-

ney King—strong use of force following a pursuit.[20] The thrill
and adrenaline rush of a pursuit apparently carried into the
arrest phase and resulted in "payback" for running from
the police.[21]

Thus, giving over to the thrill of the chase, the cheerful
embrace of the adrenaline high of the search and capture of
a "bad guy," can compromise other aspects of the police
role—the necessity to mediate disputes and to exercise the
craft of peacekeeping, the desire to embrace community policing, the necessity to protect citizens from excessive force.
For these reasons, the values celebrated by the adventure/
machismo normative order are increasingly challenged by
critics of the professional model of policing, a challenge that
is spawning significant resentment within the ranks of the
LAPD.

Conclusion

Although it is not formally encoded in laws or regulations,
the normative order of adventure/machismo still conditions
the territorial practices of the police and provides a powerful mechanism for imbuing those practices with meaning. In
this case, aggressive actions can mean that an officer possesses courage and strength. Further, the possession of these
characteristics means the officer is more likely to bring home
the trophy of a handcuffed felony suspect. This normative
order thus encourages the adoption of practices that can enable officers to control dangerous suspects. In enacting such
practices, officers tend to identify areas in terms of whether
they contain dangerous suspects and tend, when they are in
pursuit, to see space in tactical terms strictly conditioned by
the strategy of control and capture. Such a view implicitly
diminishes alternate conceptions of space, including those
held by the regular users of that space. Such an orientation

toward police work also diminishes aspects of the job that emphasize peacekeeping and disparages the current reform effort of community policing.

Adventurous officers thus define space in terms of finding and capturing quarry and enact aggressive maneuvers to control movements within that space. The tactical considerations central to this normative order are also endorsed by concerns regarding safety, the subject of chapter 6.

6. SAFETY AND POLICE TERRITORIALITY

*THERE ARE A FEW APARTMENT buildings in the central sec-
tion of the division that attract regular attention from Wilshire officers because they have long been understood to house members of various gangs. One of these apartment buildings, built
around a large central courtyard, is reportedly the original "hood"
of Los Carnales, a Latino gang whose presence is now most
significant in Hollywood. Still, groups of young people gathered outside this building are likely to attract police attention.*

*A particularly large crowd milling about the front of the
building on a Saturday night prompts a pair of passing patrol
officers to stop and investigate. As the car stops, many of the
people drift into the interior courtyard. One young man, as he
retreats, reaches toward his waist, as if to indicate that he is
"packing" a gun. The officers follow him into the courtyard,
where the young man quickly blends into a still larger crowd.
At this point, realizing that they are significantly outnumbered
and on unfamiliar ground, the two officers retreat.*

In this instance, concerns about officer safety outweigh the challenge of corralling a hostile and possibly armed individual. Regardless of the potential satisfaction of entering this scene and successfully controlling it, the officers quickly realize that their safety is compromised and beat a hasty retreat. The pull of adventure is suppressed by concerns about safety.

This illustrates just one of the many situations in which the normative order of safety significantly determines how officers view and attempt to control space. This order in part works to temper the derring-do of more adventurous actions; it consists of numerous rules and practices that seek to ensure that officers "get to go home" at the end of each shift. Indeed, getting to go home at the end of watch is the central value at the heart of this normative order and provides the principal rationale for many actions the police regularly undertake.

The importance of safety is quickly obvious to an observer of the police. Roll calls regularly end with the admonishment to "stay safe out there," and officers at the end of a watch express satisfaction that they have returned safely. Field training officers encourage new officers to make safety considerations a priority. A common folk saying around the department holds that "it is better to be judged by twelve than carried by six"—it is better to take an action that guarantees the preservation of your life even if it results in criminal action against you.[1] In these various subtle yet powerful ways, officers are admonished to take considerations of safety seriously and to act accordingly.

In this chapter I outline many actions officers take in accordance with the normative order of safety. Considerations of safety, as I explain in the first section, prompt a number of tactics the police use to attempt to secure areas they patrol, including regular reliance on the oversight capacity of helicopters. Safety concerns also explain how officers define different areas of the division, as I discuss in the second section.

The chief distinction here is between areas that are "pro-police" and those that are "anti-police"; as might be expected, it is in the latter areas that officers are most careful. Of particular concern in these areas is the threat of ambush. Finally, ideas about safety have various implications for how officers relate to the members of the communities that they patrol; I discuss these implications in the third section of the chapter.

The Practices of Safe Patrol

The imperative of staying safe requires officers to think carefully about where and how they patrol, about how they position themselves vis-à-vis potentially dangerous suspects, about how they approach and handle those suspects. It requires officers to be aware of as many aspects of the unfolding situation as possible and of the location and activities of other officers. Much emphasis is placed on properly positioning oneself, especially in relation to any possibly antagonistic foe. Emphasis is also placed on providing fellow officers with information about one's location and about the situation as it unfolds. The various rules aimed at ensuring safety thus encourage officers to be acutely aware of their environment and of their own positioning within that environment.

When officers are requested to respond to a potentially dangerous situation, their first act is to consult their mobile display terminal, an in-car device that enables access to various databases. In such an instance, the officers will want to access the information the 911 operator has gathered on the incident. (When dispatchers assign a call, they radio the number of the incident. The officers then use that number to access the incident report.) The officers are especially interested in the potential dangerousness of the suspect and in identifying characteristics. They also want to know whether the

suspect is still on the scene or whether and in what direction
the suspect left. The importance of this information is obvious: it helps the officers plan the best approach to the scene
and helps them focus their attention on a particular individual. For equally obvious reasons, officers are especially interested in knowing whether and how the suspect is armed.[2]

Depending on the situation, officers will tactically position
themselves in different ways. When the call is not serious,
questions of position are irrelevant. However, if a suspect is
possibly armed and inside a building with other people, officers may be concerned that the suspect will take hostages.
Then they will park their car on the same side of the street
as the location and a couple of doors away, so that their
presence is undetected. They wish, in this situation, to surprise
the suspect and thus prevent him from grabbing a hostage.

> *The dispatcher radios a call regarding a ringing burglary alarm
> at a natural foods store. The sergeant is headed to lunch, but
> the call is only a few blocks away. The store is undoubtedly open,
> so a burglar is likely to be confronting workers and customers.
> The store's street number is not marked, so the sergeant struggles
> to locate it. His effort to pin down the location leads him to drive
> past the store, turn around, and pass it yet again from the other
> direction. He finally determines which store it must be. He parks
> in the alley behind the store, retrieves his shotgun from the rack
> along the front seat, and instructs his ride-along to assume a
> safe position across the street in the alcove of a doorway. He
> then inches alongside the building until he reaches a window
> looking into the store. He attracts the attention of a clerk and
> uses hand signals to determine that no burglary is in progress.*

The sergeant is later critical of himself for passing by the
store twice which invites a burglar to take a hostage. Once he
parks, in a secluded alley away from the store's windows, the
sergeant's movements are designed to ensure his own safety

and that of the customers and staff. He arms himself with his most powerful weapon, the shotgun, in an attempt to ensure that he can exercise superior force should a confrontation occur. He sidles up slowly to the building and looks cautiously into the store through a window. From that position, he makes surreptitious hand movements to a clerk to determine whether a robbery is indeed occurring, but in a manner meant to prevent a robber from detecting the presence of the police. This series of tactical positionings is designed to ensure that the officer has the upper hand and is able to act first and decisively should the situation warrant. The officer conceals himself so that the element of surprise remains within his control.[3] Such situations also require safety-concerned officers to maintain good lines of sight in order to see as much of a scene as possible.[4] It is further important that officers position themselves so that all who may threaten them are in front of them; they thereby reduce the threat of an ambush.

The sergeant chose to arm himself heavily for this particular call. He saw the shotgun as his best opportunity to inflict a crippling injury should the suspect attack him or others. This is a practice frequently adopted by LAPD officers on suspected robberies and burglaries. Some officers, however, caution that injecting a gun into a situation can inflame tensions and create a greater chance for violence. One sergeant, for example, maintained that much can be accomplished by an officer who is in a secure position of cover and can invoke a strong command voice. The officer is well protected and can create the impression, with an assertive voice, that the suspect is outnumbered or outflanked and that surrender is advisable. This less direct show of force, he reasons, is more effective and lessens the risk of gunplay.

Even with his shotgun, however, the sergeant who responded to the alarm at the health food store tried to remain shielded. He walked along the edge of the building and peered only slowly into the window. This practice of walking along the edge of buildings is a habit among LAPD officers, and they teach it to ride-alongs. On two calls when officers feared guns might be involved, sergeants instructed me to move from the street, where I had been standing, to the side of the building where the officers were gathered. And when officers approach windows, they either look in surreptitiously or duck beneath them.

Safety-conscious officers want to be able to contain and control any suspect that they might confront. This conditions officers' actions when they come into contact with suspects. Suspects are searched immediately to ensure that they possess no means to harm the officers or to take control of the situation, and officers regularly handcuff suspects they fear may become violent. Thus, males in domestic disputes and unruly drunks are frequently handcuffed to prevent them from causing a disruption that not only would make the situation difficult to control but also could threaten the safety of others. In many cases officers focus not solely on the immediate suspect, but also on everyone in the suspect's party.

The sergeant hears on the radio that a "code 6 Charles" has been issued on the driver of a car detained by an officer. The term means that the suspect may have an outstanding felony warrant and should be handled accordingly.[5] Because felony suspects are often considered dangerous, the sergeant decides to provide backup. When he arrives at the scene, he finds one of the officers watching the driver of the car, who is standing on the sidewalk. The other officer is in the patrol car, located behind the suspect's car, and is using the mobile display terminal to determine more clearly whether there is indeed an outstanding warrant for the suspect. The officer in the car emerges and walks toward the suspect's car to check the vehicle identification number on the dashboard. As she walks toward the suspect's car, the sergeant pulls his flashlight into one hand and shines it into the car. His other hand rests on his gun. The officer writes down the identification number and returns to the patrol car. When she emerges a second time, the sergeant suggests to her that, in the future, she should require all the passengers to get out of the car. There are he says, three "gangster-looking" guys in the back seat, any of whom might be willing to surprise her.

In this situation, the sergeant is more concerned with safety issues than the patrol officer is. He shines his flashlight into the backseat, ensures ready access to his gun, and admonishes the officer to be more careful in the future. He encourages her to secure control over the suspects' potential movements by ordering them from the car and onto the sidewalk. If she locates them in this way, he reasons, she can better monitor any threats they might make to her safety. The larger aim is clear: to position all potential threats to safety so that their actions are more easily seen and controlled.

Proper positioning of suspects and officers is one of the best means by which officers can ensure that they do not unwittingly enter a dangerous situation. It is also a good means to ensure that officers work in coordinated fashion to prevent any undue harm from each other.

An officer on patrol near Smiley and Hauser radios that his car may have been struck by a gunshot. The sergeant on patrol responds immediately, not by proceeding directly to the last reported location of the patrol car, but by circling the area at a distance of two or three blocks. He does not want too many cars in the "kill zone," where the gang members may be concentrating their attention. Cars in the "kill zone" not only may be vulnerable to ambush, but also may place themselves in such a way that they fall victim to "friendly fire" — officers may inadvertently shoot each other in the effort to shoot a suspect.

Another sergeant enjoys eating lunch at a local hamburger stand not just because the food is good and cheap, but also be-

*cause it allows him to eat "tactically": the stand's parking lot is
at the rear of the building, and a fence runs along one side. He
can thus lay his food out on the hood of his car and stand with
his back next to the fence. He is protected by the building on
his right and the fence behind him, and thus he eats his lunch in
relative calm.*

The spatial positioning of officers — the territorial tactics
of command and control — is clearly shaped by concerns of
safety. Officers survey a situation and coordinate their collective movements to secure territorial control. These efforts
are augmented by help from helicopters.

Helicopters and the Surveillance of Space

Helicopters are a relatively new aspect of the patrol operations of the LAPD. Although they were not widely used until the mid-1970s, they are now integrated into daily operations. For all but the early-morning hours, at least one and
up to three LAPD helicopters are aloft and available to assist officers. In many cases, concerns for officer safety motivate requests for helicopter support. This is most obvious in
pursuits, when officers wish to know about traffic on the
streets they cross while they are chasing a suspect. The helicopter provides information that reduces the possibility of a
collision with an unsuspecting motorist. Helicopters are also
useful to officers worried about potential snipers or ambushes
in dark or confined spaces.

For their part, officers in the helicopter endeavor to be the
first at the scene so that they can apprise responding patrol
cars of the situation and help the officers position themselves
most safely and effectively. In January 1994, for example, an
LAPD officer was fatally shot by a young San Fernando Valley man who laid in wait for officers behind a hedge.[6] On that
night, heavy fog prevented the helicopters from providing sur-

veillance. In talking about the incident a week later, one Air Support officer expressed tremendous sadness that the fog prevented the helicopter from informing the responding officers of the sniper's location.

Helicopters are especially helpful in situations that result in perimeters; the larger perspective afforded by the helicopter provides an ability to create the most solid boundary around an elusive suspect. This not only helps ensure the eventual capture of the suspect but also restricts the suspect's capacity to surprise the officers. In some cases, a pursuit may end before officers can surround a suspect. In these situations, helicopter observers frequently radio responding patrol cars not to approach the stopped car directly for fear of an attack from those inside.

Officers may request helicopter assistance in determining how to deploy. In one situation, a group of patrol cars were responding to a report of a bank robbery. When an air unit acknowledged a response, a lieutenant who was part of the group of responding officers requested advice on how to coordinate the cars to seal the area around the bank. Each patrol car has a "shop number" on its roof, clearly visible to those in the helicopter, so that it is easy to instruct officers how to position themselves.

In another situation, officers were responding to reports of a large late-night party in a public park. Rather than immediately enter the area, the officers waited until the helicopter, using its powerful nightsun, was able to assess the size, position, and unruliness of the crowd. In this case, the nightsun was sufficient to convince the crowd to scatter, so the patrol cars left the scene.

Helicopter officers frequently use their surveillance capacity to assess not only the precise location of the call but the immediate vicinity as well. They provide information about unusual movements in the front or back of buildings, or in the surrounding block(s). They can also monitor anyone who leaves a location before the patrol cars arrive. On one call about a disturbance involving a gun, the helicopter officers succeeded in being first at the scene and watched while a young man left in a car, only to park two blocks away. They watched the young man walk into and out of a liquor store, after which a patrol car was able to stop him for questioning.

The superior speed of the helicopter was obvious on this call. The responding patrol car was mired in late-afternoon traffic while the helicopter remained in its holding pattern and observed the young man.

These advantages of speed and oversight explain the readiness with which patrol officers request helicopter assistance; anxious for information about potential danger, officers draw on the unique perspective of the helicopter to position themselves most safety and effectively. To be located properly, to be positioned tactically, is to promote safety.

Positioning and Safety

Questions of positioning, it should now be clear, lie at the heart of the safety practices endorsed by police officers. Just as it is important to be positioned appropriately vis-à-vis both potential suspects and other officers, it is also important for officers to inform others of their location so that assistance can be directed appropriately. Officers concerned with safety therefore make sure that the dispatcher is regularly updated on their location. They also make sure that they are themselves aware of where they are so that they can direct help to the proper place. For this reason, training officers often quiz trainees at random moments to make sure they develop the habit of knowing their location at all times. Veteran officers claim that in the past, training officers also required trainees to monitor the locations of all other units in the division so that they could respond with geographic correctness to a call for help.[7] The importance of knowing one's location explains the scorn officers heaped on a fellow officer who was known to fall asleep regularly. In one scenario repeated around the station, the sleep-prone officer's partner dashed from the car to chase a suspect on foot. The officer was suddenly awakened but was unable to inform other units of their location. As a result, the safety of the officer on the foot pursuit was compromised because help could not be dispatched to the proper location.

The value of knowing an officer's location is endorsed by various practices of the Communications Division, which is responsible for assigning calls to officers and for keeping track of their movements. For instance, if an officer receives a "code 6 Charles," the officer's location is immediately requested. As the call proceeds, the dispatcher receives regular reminders from the communications system to request updates from the officer. Felony suspects are considered dangerous, and suspects nabbed with a code 6 Charles have already demonstrated, with their outstanding warrant, a desire to escape the judicial system. In other words, their potential desire to flee represents another possible threat to officer safety and thus motivates the regular monitoring of the situation.

The communication between dispatcher and patrol officer is also considered crucial during vehicle pursuits, when dispatchers monitor the pursuing vehicle's location. Officers are told to stay off the radio so that the pursuing officer can provide regular updates. This helps responding vehicles know precisely where to go.

The dispatcher is monitoring the progress of a foot pursuit. The officer attempts to radio his location as he maintains the

pursuit. In their eagerness to assist, several patrol vehicles ra-
dio that they are en route. The dispatcher is angered, and pro-
nouncedly says, "For officer safety, only the pursuing officer
should respond." Her invocation of the cherished value of
safety silences the other officers.

The normative order of safety clearly influences the tactical movements of police officers. Tactics are a topic of regular conversation around the division, especially during roll call, part of which is devoted to training. There is some review of department-endorsed procedure and sometimes reviews of recent events in the division such as pursuits, officer-involved shootings, and so on. In each case, tactics are discussed extensively. Watch commanders regularly remind officers that the time to think through tactical maneuvers is during quiet moments, because in quickly unfolding situations careful review of potential courses of action is impossible. This emphasis on tactics not only helps officers ensure their safety but also buttresses their sense of themselves as strong and competent; as one watch commander pointed out, the "thugs" may be well armed, but their tactics are poor compared to those of the police. Indeed, many officers believe that, even when they are outnumbered or outarmed, they can control suspects with well-designed tactics.

In sum, the normative order of safety conditions officers to approach situations carefully, to monitor and control suspects effectively, to coordinate with other officers efficiently. It thus strongly determines how officers will move through space to ensure their own preservation. Further, it also shapes how officers define the areas they patrol. The major distinction in this context is between areas that are "pro-police" and those that are "anti-police." Different tactics are appropriate for these different areas.

Pro-police versus Anti-police Areas

*Two CRASH sergeants are chatting amiably as they drive from
their station in West Los Angeles into the Wilshire Division.
Their attention is on each other and their conversation, and
they pay little mind to the area they pass through. However, as
they get within a few blocks of their first stop, four square
blocks known as the home of an African-American gang called
the Schoolyard Crips, their behavior changes. At the same moment, without any apparent cue, both officers roll down their
windows and release their seat belts. They are about to enter
an anti-police area.*

The area is a gang hangout, so it is by definition anti-police. Gang members are seen as diametrically opposed to the
police; they are the "other" against whom officers define
themselves in sharpest distinction. To enter a gang area is to
enter a zone in which the danger to officers is most pronounced. This explains why they rolled down the windows
and released the seat belts. Both actions are seen as maximizing officer safety. They want to be able to hear any noise —
a shout, a loud footstep — that indicates an imminent threat,
and they don't want their mobility to be restricted should they
suddenly need to duck or leave the car. By rolling down their
windows and releasing the seat belts, the officers indicate that
they have passed an important geographical boundary between an area that represents no threat and one that is dangerous because it houses people who are, in their minds, anti-
police.[8] In these areas, officers must be on constant alert. By
contrast, pro-police areas allow a greater degree of relaxation.

Pro-police Areas

*It is a quiet weekday afternoon, with few calls broadcast on the
radio. The sergeant is patrolling exclusively in the Hancock*

Park area, a quiet, wealthy residential neighborhood that is the
source of very few calls even on a busy day. This is my first
time with this sergeant. Previous ride-alongs with other
sergeants involved many trips to the Smiley and Hauser area.
When I asked why he, too, did not head to Smiley and Hauser,
the officer merely gestured toward the residences he was pass-
ing. Why not, he asked, patrol where it is pleasant?

In this situation, the sergeant is enjoying the peace of the
afternoon by remaining in an area in which he is unlikely to
encounter any trouble. Not only will there be few requests for
assistance, but the people he does encounter will greet him
with a smile and a friendly wave. Further, people in pro-police areas are to be trusted.

The trail of a potential burglary suspect carries a group of
patrol officers into a middle-class residential neighborhood. One
of the officers, providing an update of the situation on the radio,
informs his audience that they are questioning residents, but
with little luck. He does say, however, "People here, they want
to see the police."

With these words, the officer communicates the message
that the residents' lack of information is genuine. In pro-police areas, residents work cooperatively with the police and
do all they can to assist the officers. In anti-police areas, by
contrast, ignorance might be interpreted as feigned, as a deliberate attempt to obstruct police efforts to nab a felon.

The quiet of a pro-police area and the possibility for cor-
dial and constructive encounters are valued by many officers.
Others, however, especially those interested in adventure, are
more likely to prefer patrolling in anti-police areas. In these
locations, the premium on officer safety demands an atten-
tiveness to tactics and position that presents a challenge adventurous officers enjoy.

Anti-police Areas

On patrol on a quiet weekday night, the sergeant decides to cruise toward Smiley and Hauser. The radio is quiet and the sergeant seems restless; he hopes that the "Smauser," as he calls it, will provide some measure of interest. The sergeant has not responded to a call and has not communicated with the dispatcher in nearly an hour. As a result, the dispatcher's last known location for the sergeant is an address in the north central part of the division. In the interim, the sergeant has seen no reason to update his location. As he gets within a few blocks of the notorious street corner, however, he slows the car and punches his location into his mobile display terminal. He also releases the safety latch on his shotgun.

The sergeant's actions illustrate the safety-oriented practices officers adopt as they approach an area they consider anti-police. The sergeant has quietly cruised much of the division for nearly an hour but has felt no need to locate himself for the dispatcher. That he chooses to do so as he enters the Smiley-Hauser area indicates that he anticipates the possibility of danger there, and he wants other units to be able to respond quickly and appropriately should trouble befall him. The release of the shotgun similarly indicates anticipation of possible danger; he wants to be able to have easy access to his most powerful weapon should the situation, in police lingo, "go sideways."

The anti-police reputation of Smiley and Hauser helps explain why some sergeants prefer to patrol in Hancock Park. These sergeants reason that, because they ride alone, they could easily get in trouble and, without a partner, would be especially vulnerable to ambush. This vulnerability is increased if there is a ride-along in the car with them. Many sergeants were unafraid to bring a ride-along with them to Smiley and Hauser, but one encouraged me to release my seat belt and another gave a quick lesson on using the radio so that I could seek help if necessary. The latter sergeant promised that if I radioed that an officer needed help at Smiley and Hauser, that other units would be there in a "nanosecond," presumably because of the reputation of the area. Still another sergeant, who was new to the division, repeated aloud each cross street he passed, the better to ensure assistance should he need it; he could radio for help to his precise location.

Smiley and Hauser has earned its reputation not just because it is home to two gangs, but also because members of one of those gangs had shot at Wilshire officers on two different occasions in the previous year. One of those incidents occurred just a week before my fieldwork began, so the area was much talked about and reviled by the officers. Those incidents helped the officers define the area as anti-police and thus motivated actions to ensure their maximum ability to seek help and to help themselves should trouble arise.

The definition of an area as anti-police, then, has implications for the practices officers adopt when they enter that area. They act to increase their ability to monitor and respond to a hostile situation, and to receive swift assistance should it prove necessary. Once a situation develops, the fact that the area is anti-police also affects how officers react, since they recognize that citizen cooperation is not assured.

At roll call, the sergeant serving as watch commander is engaging the officers in a discussion of a fight the previous night between an officer and a civilian. The incident began with a report of a drive-by shooting. A car suspected to have been involved in the shooting was detained by a patrol car. As soon as the car stopped, the two young men in the front seats quickly opened their doors and fled, leaving three others in the backseat. The two who fled caught the police by surprise and possessed such an advantage that the officers did not give chase. Instead,

*they commanded the remaining three to get out of the car, and
they waited for help from other officers, which arrived swiftly.*

*All of the youths were Latino, and the events became the
subject of much attention from many other Latinos who live in
the neighborhood. One of the suspects spoke to the crowd in
Spanish and claimed his innocence. He further encouraged the
crowd to pressure the police to let him go. The crowd obliged.
Two in the crowd were especially assertive and thus drew the
enmity of one of the officers at the scene. The officer eventually
threatened to use physical force on the two if they did not keep
quiet. The two did not desist, and the officer, after a short tussle, handcuffed them.*

*In the review of the incident, several are critical of the offi-
cer's actions. Someone suggests that threatening the two men
in front of a crowd of neighbors was not smart because it makes
it harder for them to back down; they stand to lose face should
they accede to the officer's request. Another officer believes
strongly that the situation should not have reached that point
in the first place. He argues that as soon as the crowd began to
gather, the officers should have quickly hustled all the suspects
to the station and sorted things out there. He believes it is vi-
tally important not to allow a crowd to get involved in an incident, because that can make the situation unmanageable.*

This incident illustrates how an anti-police crowd can, from
the police perspective, make a situation troublesome and
therefore a potential threat to their safety. Incited by a suspect who felt wrongly accused, the crowd began "chipping"
at the police and thus angered an officer who felt needlessly
challenged. So angered, the officer responded in a way that
was not sensitive to the environment in which the young men
found themselves; he challenged them, and, in the public eye,
they felt compelled to stand their ground. A tussle ensued,
but critical fellow officers believe it was senseless and pre-
ventable. The officers at the scene, according to this criticism,
failed to recognize the threat to their safety posed by the anti-

police crowd and failed to act quickly to remove themselves to their own turf, the station, where they could exercise control.

Anti-police areas pose clear threats, in the eyes of the officers, to their capacity to control situations and thus to their capacity to ensure their own safety. Concerns about safety in anti-police areas may further lead officers to feel as if the legal rules regarding detentions and searches are subject to bending.

> *Roll call training concerns the legal rules regarding detaining citizens in public space. After reviewing the basic legal rules, the sergeant in charge of the training reads three scenarios and asks the officers whether a detention is legally permissible. In the second of these scenarios, the officer is said to have spied a "dirtbag" and stopped the man to search and question him. One of the patrol officers points out that the word dirtbag is a dead giveaway that the stop was not motivated by legally defensible reasons. The officer goes on to say, however, that if the suspect was dressed a particular way, or was acting like he was engaged in narcotics activity, or was in a particular area, a stop could be justified. When the officer says "particular area," another officer immediately pipes up with "Smiley and Hauser," to the approving murmurs of the crowd.*

This discussion makes clear that the significance of Smiley and Hauser to the officers heightens the importance of ensuring their own safety in that area, even if it means stepping past legal restrictions on their ability to detain citizens. It is clear that the officers believe that the location itself justifies their concern about safety and thus should allow them to escape a strict enforcement of laws that otherwise might restrict their capacity to control what, in their eyes, might be a dangerous suspect.

The most extreme fear of officers in anti-police areas is the possibility of an ambush.

Avoiding Ambushes

It is about two weeks after an officer has been shot near Smiley and Hauser. The sergeant is committed to providing the area what he sarcastically refers to as some "positive police attention." Specifically, he marshals a group of eight officers to approach a particular apartment building on foot. Several alleged gang members regularly gather in front of the building, and at least one of them, the sergeant is convinced, knows the identities of the shooters. He wants the officers to gather identification on those hanging out in front of the building and see if any have outstanding warrants. If they do, the officers can arrest them as a way of convincing them to "give up" the identity of the shooters.

The officers park their cars about a block away so that they can surprise the group at the apartment building. As he walks away from his car, the sergeant, already several steps behind the others, realizes that he has not locked his car door. I volunteer to walk back and lock it. The sergeant hesitates, but accepts my offer. He heads off to the scene, where I join him a moment later.

After the officers question the men and arrest one on an outstanding warrant, the sergeant and I walk back to the car. Two patrol officers walk alongside us, both with their guns in their hands. They are escorting us back to our car, the sergeant explains, because now is the time that "they can set up on you."

Once we are safely back in the car, the sergeant prepares to head out when he hears the loud screeching of tires. He speeds toward the sound and sees a car at the end of a dead-end street with its brake lights on. The sergeant chooses not to pursue the car even though he is suspicious that it is the source of the screeching noise.

The fear of ambush motivates the tactical decisions of the sergeant and the other officers. It explains the heavily armed escort back to the sergeant's car and his decision not to enter a dead-end street to chase a suspicious car. In both cases, his definition of the area as resolutely anti-police means that his sensitivity to the potential for an ambush is high. It also explains his later apology for allowing me to traverse the street unprotected when I returned to lock the patrol car and then walked to the apartment building alone.[9]

Officers remind each other to remain aware of the potential for ambushes. At a roll-call training the day after a nearly fatal shooting of a CRASH officer in another division, the officers reviewed some safety measures. Officers should be suspicious, for example, if police assistance is requested on a 911 call from a pay phone, particularly one located in an anti-police area.[10] They should also be suspicious if they respond to a call on a normally crowded street only to discover that the street is empty. Some officers simply suggest that they rely on their instinct to assess situations where something "doesn't feel right," when "the hair stands up on the back of your neck."

Because of the potentially lethal dangers imminent in situations such as these, it is easy to understand why the normative order of safety is invoked so regularly by the police, why it exerts a powerful influence on how officers make and mark space. However, there is reason to assess this order critically; it was a particular concern of the Christopher Commission's assessment of the LAPD uses of force.[11]

Safety and the Potential Excesses of the Police

The LAPD's strong focus on safety emerged as a central concern of the Christopher Commission, which was established in the wake of the Rodney King incident to examine uses of force by the department's officers. The commission's report drew a link between the concern for safety and the level of tension between the police and the community. Because the department, and especially the training officers who exercise so much influence over new officers, so pronouncedly stress safety, young officers quickly develop a we/they mentality, the report suggested. By emphasizing the threat posed by suspicious people in the community, officers easily group people together and label them "anti-police." Once they are labeled, people may no longer get careful and considered treatment at the hands of the police. In other words, the Christopher Commission feared that the preeminent focus on safety made it easier for officers to develop a siege mentality and, from there, to lose the capacity to differentiate real from imagined threats and to respond in measured fashion in actually facing a threat. And because "anti-police" areas are invariably dominated by blacks and Latinos, police abuses fall disproportionately onto those groups.

A sense of being under siege did seem to be present in the Wilshire Division. During my fieldwork, the division's parking lot was undergoing reconstruction and officers were forced to park their cars in a lot about a block from the station. Because the Schoolyard Crips' territory is located immediately across from the station, the officers felt it necessary to post an officer in the parking lot at all times to protect their cars. Even when the division acquired permission to use the parking lot of a bank located next door to the station, the practice of posting a patrol car continued. It was clear, in other words, that the officers felt a significant threat from the "knuckleheads" who lived across the street.[12]

A siege mentality seems to influence how officers view an area such as Smiley and Hauser. Some officers even complained that many of their colleagues have difficulty differentiating people in that area, and thus tend to feel threatened by everyone they see there. It is therefore reasonable to concur with the concerns of the Christopher Commission that an overemphasis on safety can increase the potential of unnecessarily harsh police actions.

Concerns about safety also lie beneath the strong sense of esprit de corps among the officers. For example, I was observing the Communications Division on the night of the nearly fatal shooting of a CRASH officer. The dispatcher informed me later that more than sixty-five patrol units had responded to that call, in addition to the K-9 units and SWAT. The dispatcher, though she was disappointed that she had fewer units to assign calls to, was philosophic about it: "You know," she said, "no one can tell them not to go." She was aware that the officers' collective need to feel protected in part motivated their massive response to the shooting. This need for protection is also invoked by officers to explain their oft-noted "code of silence," which shields abusers from supervisors. Officers argue that if they "snitch off" one of their peers, they cannot expect effective backup on dangerous calls. In these cases, concerns for safety inhibit the sensible deployment of resources and the capacity to oversee officer conduct.

On the other hand, police concern about safety is understandable, particularly in an area where police have been ambushed. It is impossible to imagine how an officer would not be especially careful while on patrol there. It is clear, though, that safety considerations carried to an extreme can exacerbate the officers' sense of themselves as less-than-powerful victims of forces out to get them and can thereby increase the possibility that they will lash out inappropriately. Thus, while the definition of pro- versus anti-police areas is perhaps unavoidable in an occupation in which lives are indeed lost, it is important that these definitions be nuanced and open to reconsideration. Otherwise, citizens may fall victim to unnecessary uses of force, and police-community relations may wither.

Conclusion

This chapter makes clear how considerations of safety influence the territorial practices of the police. Motivated by a desire to make sure they return safely home at the end of each shift, officers think carefully about where they are and how they are positioned. They attempt to position themselves so that they retain the element of surprise in encounters with potentially dangerous suspects and maintain the largest possible perspective on each situation as it unfolds. They try to be aware of their location at all times so they can get immediate help if necessary. They endeavor to coordinate their activities effectively should trouble erupt. To be properly positioned and clearly locatable is to act in accordance with the normative order of safety.

This order also leads officers to define the areas they patrol as pro- and anti-police. Officers concerned with the need to be able to respond swiftly and powerfully to hostile actions approach areas in the latter category with particular care. The distinction may, however, cloud officers' ability to respond in a nuanced and measured fashion to potential threats in areas they consider to be anti-police.

It should now be clear that the capacity to control an area is of immense importance to officers in preserving their own safety. Controlling an area is also important to officers who want to demonstrate to their peers that they are competent. We now turn to a discussion of the normative order of competence.

7. COMPETENCE
IN POLICE
TERRITORIALITY

TWO SENIOR LEAD OFFICERS ARE on patrol early on a Saturday afternoon, checking various locations that have elicited complaints from residents. For the moment, they are interested in three men standing outside an apartment building on the northwest corner of an intersection. One of the men is standing alongside the street, while the other two are lounging about fifteen yards behind him in a driveway. The driver sidles the car up to the one near the street, and the officer in the passenger seat strikes up a conversation. The officers, it turns out, feel sure that the three men are engaged in drug sales, and they question the man by the street about their activities. It is clear that the officer in the passenger seat, in whose area the two are patrolling, would like to get out of the car and question the other two men as well. His partner, however, motions to me in the backseat and suggests that it would be best to stay in the car; the officer presumably does not welcome a potentially inflammable confrontation with a ride-along in tow.[1] The officer in the passen-

ger seat stays in the car and leaves the men with a warning that they should keep their noses clean.

The two officers reenter traffic and immediately turn west. When they do so, a group of young men loitering in a convenience store parking lot two doors away scatter and run. The driver guns the car into the parking lot, and the two officers jump out to detain as many of the group as possible. They capture four of the five and order them to stand with their hands behind their heads. The officers search and identify them, then run their names on the mobile display terminal for outstanding arrest warrants. The officers also comb the area thoroughly for any illicit goods the group may have discarded. Neither search bears fruit, so the officers choose to let the men go. A few of them begin walking west, but the senior lead officer responsible for the area admonishes them to go the other direction. He wants them to go east and to cross to the other side of the street, he says. He does this because the street is the boundary between Wilshire Division and Rampart Division; once they are on the other side, the men become some other officer's concern.

This example illustrates how the normative order of competence structures the territorial practices of police officers. The officers face two groups, both of which they believe are engaged in the illegal sale of drugs. In one instance they remain in their car and merely issue a warning. In the other, the officers jump from the car and detain and search the group. The more aggressive response to the second group results from that group's attempted flight. Flight not only constitutes evidence of criminal activity but also is a direct challenge to the officers' sense of competence. To allow the group to flee without a response would be an indefensible admission that they do not exercise control over the areas for which they are responsible. When a direct challenge is issued, the officers' sense of themselves as capable territorial agents demands that they jump hurriedly from the car even though, moments before, they considered it prudent to refrain from an identical action.

Officers wish to demonstrate territorial competence to two audiences. The first is the suspects they encounter; the second is other police officers. The officer demands not only that the suspects disperse but also that they leave the area for which he is responsible. He thus wants to ensure, as best he is able, that the activities in which the young men are engaged occur outside his area. To be able to police his area thus is to demonstrate his competence to his supervisors and fellow officers. The officer, in other words, wants to communicate both to suspects *and* to fellow officers that he can determine what does or does not occur in his area.

Precisely what constitutes competence varies considerably depending upon an officer's bureaucratically defined responsibilities. Further, the range of challenges officers face is so broad that simplistic rules about competence cannot apply to all instances.[2] In many situations, however, competent fulfillment of a given assignment is defined by the effective exercise of territoriality, through the demonstration of the capacity to clear areas of unwanted people and activities.

In this chapter I explain how consciousness of the two audiences—suspects and the police fraternity—shapes how officers define themselves as competent agents of territorial action. The first section addresses how officers enact territoriality as a means of corralling and controlling suspects; in these cases, the officers try to convey to suspects that they possess the ultimate authority over a given area. The second section addresses how officers at the same time enact territoriality to demonstrate their competence to other officers. Together, the two sections make clear that successful territorial actions are of fundamental importance to the officers' sense of themselves as capable, a point developed in the chapter's conclusion.

Competence and Territorial Control of Suspects

Territorial control of suspects is important to officers interested in proving their masculine prowess or in protecting themselves from harm. Such control can further demonstrate to officers that they can competently handle the job, that they can assert their authority and dominance over suspects by controlling their movements. This can mean quickly and competently erecting a perimeter to contain a suspect who is on the run. It can mean asserting a strong presence in areas where the police are challenged in an attempt to establish themselves as the dominant authority over that area. Or it can mean wiping out the territorial challenge implicit in gang graffiti. In each of these instances, officers try to enact themselves as competent wielders of police authority by maintaining their capacity to know and manipulate the territory of the suspects they pursue.

Establishing Perimeters

An officer assigned to a Z car is searching for a rape suspect. On patrol in the neighborhood where the suspect is known to hang out, the officer spies a man who fits the suspect's description. When the suspect sees the officer, he runs behind a building and disappears from view. The officer radios for help and receives it; responding units quickly position themselves on each of the four streets surrounding the reported location of the suspect. A helicopter is also summoned, and it uses a heat-detecting infrared mechanism to locate the suspect. Once he is located, the suspect is summoned at gunpoint from his hiding place, handcuffed, and taken to jail. The officers congratulate each other on how quickly they set up an impermeable perimeter, and thus how they were able to capture a suspect who attempted to flee.

The officers' sense of themselves as competent actors is reinforced by their successful tactical deployment, which contains and eventually captures an allegedly violent criminal. Despite the fact that the suspect attempts to flee, and perhaps was aware of hiding places that he assumed would escape police detection, the police gain the upper hand through teamwork and technology. Issued a direct challenge by the suspect, the police marshal their resources to reassert control through their territorial tactics. A protracted period of group congratulations reaffirms a collective sense of competence.

> A patrol team requests that a driver who has run a stop sign pull over. The driver accedes to the request but speeds off when the officers get out of their car to approach. In the time it takes the officers to return to their car, the suspect gains an insurmountable advantage; despite the eventual assistance of two other patrol units, the suspect escapes "into the wind." The sergeant supervising the chase laments the fact that the helicopter was unable to grant their request for assistance. Once the helicopter arrives, he maintains, "they don't get away."

The helicopters, in other words, not only help guarantee safety but also help ensure competence in police efforts to contain and corral suspects who otherwise can move at will through public space.

Establishing Command over Space

The creation of perimeters around fleeing suspects, often with the assistance of helicopters, is an especially intensive effort at police territorial control. But control of space is just as important in less dramatic police efforts to establish their competence.

> A sergeant happily recounts an incident that occurred the previous night at Smiley and Hauser. A group of officers had

approached some young men in front of an apartment building
the police recognize as a gang hangout. Unbeknownst to the
young men, another group of officers was positioned one block
to the south because they expected the group to flee the ap-
proaching officers. This is precisely what happened. However,
to the surprise of the police, the young men did not emerge im-
mediately south of the apartment building, but several doors to
the west. They had run, the police soon ascertained, between a
group of buildings and emerged through a hole in a fence to the
west. The officers were happy to acquire this piece of "geo-
graphical intelligence"; they planned to plug the hole in the
fence in the expectation that it would help them in the future to
contain suspects they wish to detain for questioning or arrest.

The officers' satisfaction at discovering this key piece of
"geographical intelligence" is an obvious outgrowth of their
need to feel in command of the areas they patrol, to be able
to contain suspects when they wish. They strive to possess
a strong sense that their commands for suspects to remain
in place will be obeyed and that they can overcome challenges to those commands. This sense of competence can be
challenged by any citizen who refuses to respond to a police
request.

A foot-beat team encounters a transient male standing in
front of a convenience store. Evincing obvious disgust, the two
approach the man and ask him to walk to the side of the build-
ing. Once they are there, one of the two officers begins yelling at
the man. She repeatedly asks him why he is still loitering in front
of the store when they have asked him repeatedly to leave the
area. She asks the man several times, "What does it take for
you to do as we tell you to?" She reminds him that they have
told him on four or five previous occasions to go to a store that
is not on their beat and says that his actions reveal that he
"clearly does not respect" their authority. She wonders aloud
why the man will not listen to them.

The officer claims a desire to pin a major crime on the man as a means of asserting their authority. When they run a warrant check on him, they discover an outstanding misdemeanor warrant for five hundred dollars. They decide to take him in for an "attitude adjustment." One of the officers admits that the first few times they encountered the man they felt no need to arrest him; because he has ignored their requests that he relocate, they are asserting their authority.

In this scenario, the officers are acting within their legal authority by arresting the man for an outstanding warrant. They are further acting in accord with the wishes of the owner of the convenience store. However, they are also acting to thwart an implicit if understated challenge to their territorial authority. By remaining on the store's property, the man is an annoyance to potential customers but, more significantly in this context, he is also refusing to pay heed to police commands. Thus challenged by the steadfast presence of the transient, the officers resort to stronger territorial actions — they forcibly remove the man from the scene and place him in jail. This action, the officers hope, will serve as a sufficient "attitude adjustment" and convince the man to take their commands more seriously.

Of further interest in this situation is the fact that the man displayed clear signs of mental illness. He responded very slowly, if at all, to the officers' requests and spoke only in monosyllables. His eyes were glazed and did not register significant comprehension. Despite these signs of ineffective communication, the officer continued to berate the man for not showing her proper respect. Yelling at him and arresting him, in other words, appeared to meet the officer's internal need to feel respected as much as it served any public need for control of the man's movements.

This sort of temporary blindness to the reality of suspects lies behind the reputed instances of beatings following police pursuits.[3] Not only are officers in these situations often enjoying the adventurousness of the chase, they are also responding to a direct challenge to their authority. Anyone who chooses to run is refusing to recognize police power and, for that reason alone, draws the ire of officers. At stake, then, is not just the thrill of the chase or bringing a suspect to justice, but also the restoration of police authority. If they are successful in the capture, officers may be tempted to release their adrenaline on the suspect; they may use violence to convey vividly that their authority should not be challenged.

Reclaiming Turf

This rankling at challenges to police authority lies at the heart of the Wilshire officers' vilification of Smiley and Hauser. They regularly call it the worst area in the division and, if they are asked why, will usually say that officers get shot at there. This is obviously a safety concern, but it also involves competence: some of the residents refuse to accept police authority over the area and violently challenge that authority. Officers patrol the area regularly not just because of crime, but also because they feel that challenges to their authority cannot remain unanswered. Without some sort of response, the police would feel as if their competence was minimal, as if their capacity for territorial control was weak and easily overcome. This helps explain the officers' frustration with what, from their perspective, was a timid investigation into the shooting of an officer at Smiley and Hauser. The officers on regular patrol felt an immediate need to reclaim control of the area, to make it clear that their authority could be reestablished despite the most violent of challenges. The officers, in other words, did not want to look weak in the eyes of their most vilified of foes, the gang member, because it threatened their sense of competence and authority. As long as the shooter(s) remained free, police authority was implicitly understood as needlessly weak.[4]

Police officers can get frustrated if the bureaucratic structure does not effectively back them up; their authority on the street, they believe, will be compromised. The same sort of logic drives the officers' regular complaints about the judicial system. Specifically, officers complain that the suspects they capture reemerge from jail too quickly. This frustration undoubtedly reflects a conservative law-and-order approach to crime, but it also stems from their sense of themselves as competent possessors of territorial authority. The prospect of jail is one of their strongest threats, one of the most valuable cards they can play in the game of contain and control. This extreme form of territoriality—the threatened removal of a suspect from his or her home and the confinement that follows—is a significant power and thus a prized means for establishing police competence in controlling the areas they patrol. The police complain about a lax judicial system because, from their perspective, short jail terms undercut this power, and with it the officers' sense of themselves as competent. If the threat of jail becomes increasingly meaningless to suspects, then the capacity of the police to exert control becomes significantly weaker. Complaints about the judicial system, then, often express officers' frustration with what they perceive as barriers to their exercise of competent territorial control.

Graffiti as Territorial Challenge

From the police perspective, graffiti is one of the more obvious contestations of their authority. Much of this graffiti is inscribed by street gangs, and is indeed intended as a gesture of territorial dominance. The primary audience is other gang members. Some graffiti is directed at the police, but this is not necessary for police to feel challenged by it; gang messages on buildings send a clear message to officers that they do not control this space. For this reason, the Wilshire Division has a staff member devoted exclusively to graffiti whose job is to monitor and quickly erase the polluting marks of young taggers and gang members. Senior lead officers pride themselves on their ability to "stay on top of" graffiti in their areas, to erase gang attempts at territorial dominance by erasing the pen and paint markings as quickly as possible.

Graffiti also can be employed to assist police efforts to control territory. Officers who are aware of different groups' "tags" can determine which groups are challenging each other. For example, if a rival gang enters, say, the Rolling 20's turf, crosses out 20's graffiti and writes over their own tag, this is an explicit challenge to 20's control of this space. It may portend an upcoming turf battle. An attentive officer, skilled in the art of decoding graffiti, may then summon CRASH officers to establish a regular presence in the area to quell a possible outbreak of gang violence.

It is clear that an audience of primary relevance to officers interested in demonstrating their competence is the suspects the officers attempt to control. Such control demands that the police possess the capacity to locate and contain suspects, that they competently exercise their authority and overcome challenges to that authority. Police expect to hold effective sway over any public area they enter, and thus expect their commands to be obeyed. Citizens who challenge those commands must be swiftly and effectively countermanded if the police sense of competence is to remain intact. As Rubinstein starkly puts it, "For the patrolman the street is everything; if he loses that, he has surrendered his reason for being what he is."[5]

In this sense, police competence depends upon effective responses to the actions of suspects. Through those responses, officers are communicating not only to suspects but also to each other. Fellow officers, in other words, provide an important audience for whom demonstrations of competence acquire meaning.

Competence and the Fear of "Losing It"

When officers respond to a suspect's movements, they wish not only to convey to the suspect that police authority is real and worthy of respect, but also to show their fellow officers that they are able to control the areas for which they are responsible. To be unable to control an area is referred to as "losing it," a condition officers labor to avoid. Individual officers can be seen as "losing it," and so can the division as a whole. Officers responsible for a particular area often have a strong desire to demonstrate to fellow officers that they can effectively respond to problems. Similarly, officers in any given division wish to demonstrate to other divisions that they can handle the call load in their territory. Even the department as a whole wants to convey to itself that it is capable of establishing and maintaining social order; failure to do so, as in the case of the urban uprising in 1992, may lead to a significant loss of a sense of internal competence.

Individual Competence

The incident I discussed at the outset of this chapter is a good example of an individual officer striving to demonstrate his capacity to keep his area clear of unwanted activities. His admonition to the young men to cross to the other side of the street is obviously motivated by his desire that the men and their activities become the responsibility of some other po-

lice officer. Should the men persist in hanging out on his side
of the street, and in engaging in illicit activities, they would
be a visible symbol of the officer's inability to exert effective
control of his area.[6] His desire to exercise control also motivates his later discussion with his partner for the day about
how to approach the corner in the future; they decide they
will come from the rear, the better to surprise the men and
deprive them of the chance to hide contraband. If the contraband can be retrieved, then the men could be sent to jail
and the corner cleared, at least for a time.

In this case, the officer is a senior lead, whose degree of
territorial responsibility is especially high. As a senior lead,
he has a commitment to monitoring ongoing problems in the
area and to making demonstrable progress in "cleaning up"
those problems. Unlike patrol officers, who may be assigned
to different areas on different nights, senior leads develop a
more intimate knowledge of their Basic Car Areas, because
they have a more clearly defined bureaucratic responsibility
for the concerns of their area. But even regular patrol car officers report a sense of frustration, even shame, when they do
not know well the areas to which they are assigned. They
dislike, for example, needing to use a map to find the location of a call; this is a visible symbol not only of their potential vulnerability (given the importance of always knowing
one's location) but also of a weak point in their sense of competence. If the area is so unfamiliar that officers cannot easily locate themselves, it is unlikely that they will be able to
draw upon any local knowledge in trying to locate or contain a suspect.[7]

Territorial control, it is believed, can be maximized if officers are deeply aware of the areas they patrol and if they possess keen powers of observation. This can mean developing
a knowledge of likely escape routes and hiding places, and of

hangouts of potential suspects. It can mean learning something of the social network surrounding a group of potential suspects to provide avenues for investigation. It can mean knowing which suspects are potentially dangerous and thus require a particularly careful approach. And it can mean recognizing the clothing, demeanor, and movements of people who may be involved in criminal activity.

All of these valued pieces of knowledge require officers to patrol an area extensively and with a sharp eye. Veteran officers in the department, however, believe that the art of "observational policing," the capacity to detect evidence of criminal activity from the barest of clues, is a dying art in the LAPD. They place much of the blame for this on officers' reliance on the mobile display terminal and the information it provides rather than on what they gather themselves. By this logic, officers have become somewhat lazy in exercising their powers of observation.[8] Officer "investigations" increasingly consist of using the databases available on their terminals. This typically means running checks either on a potential suspect's license plates, to see if a car is stolen, or on a suspect's name and identifying characteristics, to determine whether there are any outstanding warrants for him or her. In sum, LAPD officers are less likely, according to this line of thought, to pay close attention to their environment and use their own sleuthing abilities to detect evidence of criminality. As one sergeant summarized, too many officers increasingly "drive with their windows closed and their eyes straight ahead."

Still, the phrase "good obs" is heard regularly, indicating the continued valuing of keen observation, which can lead to the most competent police work. This often means measuring an observed action against the environment in which it occurs. One sergeant, for example, recalled an incident in which he captured a fleeing burglar in a neighborhood with a labyrinthine street pattern. The driver of the car, he observed, clearly telegraphed his lack of familiarity with the area: he wasn't able to navigate its complexity.

Officers who want to corral robbers in the northeast area of the division say that they look for various telltale signs, such as slowly moving cars, cars that are double-parked, or cars with one or two passengers that are parked around the corner from a street with heavy traffic. Those in such cars could be either looking for potential victims or positioning themselves for speedy getaways.

And even if officers do rely on their mobile terminals to assist them in discovering, say, stolen cars, their success will depend on their ability to read various signs: punched locks, license plates dirtier or cleaner than the car, plates from car dealers who sell a different make of car, and so on.

Demonstrating the capacity to control one's area, often through effective observational policing, can mean controlling not only hostile suspects, but fellow officers as well. Many officers, for example, like to patrol A91, where there are many arrestable people. An officer assigned to patrol A91 may witness "poaching" — other officers swooping into the area looking for felony arrests. Poaching is often understood as an affront to the officers responsible for the area and implicitly makes the poacher's area some other car's responsibility. This is especially true if the poacher succeeds in making an arrest; processing will detain the car for an hour or two. Officers exert verbal pressure on colleagues who are prone to poaching.[9]

Division Competence

The police sense of territorial competence is even more vividly experienced by an officer as a member of a division. In this context, it is important that the division as a whole work to prevent outside units from needing to enter. This means, in effect, responding to calls quickly enough so that a backlog does not develop. If outside units are regularly called in, then the division's reputation in the department is threatened, a possibility that officers do not relish. When outside units are needed, the division is said to be "dropping calls," a vivid evocation of a loss of internal control. In such a situation, sergeants, who normally are not dispatched on calls, will begin volunteering to take calls, especially those that outside units have agreed to handle. At all ranks, then, officers work to preserve the division's reputation by ensuring that outside units are not necessary.

> *A dispatcher assigned to the Wilshire Division is unable to get any officers to respond to her request for a unit to handle a domestic dispute. She cannot simply assign it to a unit, because all of them are officially engaged with an ongoing call. She makes a general broadcast in hopes that one of them is about to clear and can assume responsibility for this high-priority call. Nobody bites. She decides to try to fake them out. She comes onto the Wilshire frequency and appears to assign the call to a Hollywood car. In fact, she is not speaking on the Hollywood frequency, and thus is not actually assigning the call. Her ploy works: within seconds, a Wilshire patrol unit accepts the call and orders the Hollywood car out of the division. The dispatcher claps her hands in delight.*

The dispatcher is aware of divisional pride and manipulates it to get a Wilshire unit to respond to a high-priority call. Led to believe that an outside unit is coming into the division, a Wilshire officer accepts the call to prevent damage to the division's reputation in the department. The dispatcher cleverly plays on the officers' collective definition of competence to entice a unit to clear its call and head to the domestic dispute.[10]

The dispatcher's ability to mobilize the unit is obviously abetted by the public nature of the radio. All officers quickly learn how to decode radio messages to learn what their colleagues are or are not doing. The Basic Car to which an officer is assigned has its own moniker, which is used for radio communications. All of the Wilshire Basic Cars have the same two-character "prefix": 7A. The 7 identifies the Wilshire Division to all department personnel (the Hollywood Division is 6, the Rampart Division 4, the Pacific Division 14). The A is short for "area," and thus identifies the car as a basic patrol car. A supervisor's car is an L car (for "lone," because sergeants ride by themselves), a senior lead officer's car is an SLO car, a vice car is a V. The last part of the Basic Car's moniker refers to the area it is patrolling. Thus, 7A29 is a Basic Car responsible for an area in the northeast part of the division. Similarly, 7SLO33 is a senior lead officer responsible for the central part of the division. The primary purpose of these monikers is for all who communicate on the radio to have an easy means of identifying each car.

Implicit in this identification is awareness of the responsibilities and limitations of each car. If 7A29, for example, is assigned a call in the southwest part of the division, everyone who is listening to the radio will recognize that the pattern of assigning calls has been severely violated. If 7L30, a sergeant's car, radios that it is responding to a domestic dispute, chances are that another car will arrive at the scene as well; domestic disputes are regarded as volatile and thus too much for a single officer to handle. And if 6A63 responds to a call in Wilshire, everyone knows that a significant breach of department etiquette has occurred: the division is unable to handle its calls and has had to rely on contiguous divisions. The radio, then, serves as more than just a means for dispatching patrol cars; it is also a public arena in which competence, or lack thereof, is displayed for all to hear.

The radio dispatcher taps into a divisional pride that is threatened when outside units are needed to pick up dropped calls. This pride can also be wounded when outside units "poach" in Wilshire's territory. Some of the more active parts of the division abut boundaries with contiguous divisions and thus are prone to "raids" from those divisions. Keeping up with the internal call load and thus preventing the legitimate intrusion of outside units is a means for Wilshire officers to prevent outsiders from becoming accustomed to patrolling the division and capturing some of its felony arrests.

Department Competence

Individual officers desire to exercise control over the areas to which they are assigned and collectively desire to create a division that can handle its responsibilities without outside help. This desire for a collective sense of territorial control extends to the department as a whole. This is perhaps most obvious in the general reaction to the outbreak of civil unrest following the acquittals of the officers involved in the Rodney King beating in 1992. As I discussed in chapter 1, this helps explain the fact that Florence and Normandie became the focus of so much attention as the "flashpoint" of the rioting.

The external and internal uproar that followed the uprisings, an uproar that generated a second independent commission to investigate the LAPD, made unusually clear the expectation, both within and outside the police, that officers ultimately will be able to establish order in public places. It led to a sense within the department that it had "let the city down"[11] and created a strong determination that similar unrest would not follow if the officers were acquitted in a federal trial a year later. The department developed a new set of tactics for "unusual occurrences" and trained officers extensively before the second trial. It was obvious that the department did not want to suffer any further loss of external faith or internal sense of competence by failing to prevent civil unrest in the future.

Conclusion

The concern about the LAPD's inability to stem the unrest that boiled over at Florence and Normandie vividly reveals how the capacity to contain and control threats to public order lies at the heart of police work. Officers want to communicate to citizens and to each other that they can dictate whether and how movements occur through public space, that they can establish authority that holds ultimate sway over public actions. This sense of competence leads officers to value such actions as creating effective perimeters and "good obs" to locate a particularly dangerous criminal. It leads officers to fear the prospect of "losing it," of "dropping calls" and thereby admitting to other divisions that they cannot handle their responsibilities. And it leads the department as a whole to develop more effective means of establishing public order in the face of potential civil unrest. The normative order of competence, in other words, deeply shapes the practices and values of police territoriality.

Effective territorial action not only demonstrates to officers that they are competent, but also can contribute to their sense that they act as moral agents. In other words, officers demonstrate not just a capacity to corral suspects but also moral worth by helping rid society of the undesirable actions of "bad guys." Police territoriality is deeply undergirded by considerations of moral action, as the next chapter makes plain.

8. THE MORALITY OF POLICE TERRITORIALITY

THE MORAL ASPECTS OF STATE power are a subject of increasing scholarly interest.[1] In these discussions, the state is seen as actively involved in creating its citizens through efforts to encourage proper moral development and deportment. These processes work toward the goals of internal pacification and cohesion: the morally well developed citizen is productive and dedicated to the nation's overall welfare. This sense of internal morality can be developed through, say, particular educational efforts or various welfare programs. It can also be developed through the processes of defining a morally inferior other.[2] This process of social boundary construction has been examined in international relations work that shows how nation-states frequently define themselves as morally strong by vilifying—and often demonizing—an opposing nation-state.[3] With attention focused both inwardly on the processes of education, parenting, and general development and outwardly on the alleged inferiorities of other nations, the state, according to this line of thought, actively works to inculcate a certain morality within its citizenry. As Corrigan and Sayer summarize it: "Moral regulation is co-extensive with state formation, and state forms are always animated and legitimated by a particular moral ethos."[4]

This chapter represents an extension of the ongoing scholarly discussion about state morality. I discuss not only state actions aimed externally at the moral comportment of the citizenry but also the *internal* sense of moral rightness state actors develop to understand and justify their actions. In acting to promote what they define as the morally good, police officers attempt to reform the citizenry and, simultaneously, to construct themselves as valuable moral agents. This internal sense of morality provides a deep reservoir of meaning for police officers who regularly intervene in the lives of citizens.

The argument here, briefly, is that police territoriality is understood by the officers who enact it as a deeply moral enterprise. Ideas about right and wrong, about good and evil, influence how officers view the suspects and areas they encounter and how they understand the purpose and efficacy of their actions. These moral frameworks provide a strong sense of meaning for officers by creating an overarching means for understanding the value of their actions. Such frameworks imbue police work with a high degree of internal legitimacy and thereby provide a hedge against the ambiguity inherent in police decisions. The police often intervene in situations that are contested and difficult to comprehend, and police actions inevitably work against the interest of at least one party. An overarching, transsituational sense of goodness helps rationalize actions that do some degree of harm or are open to second-guessing. Ambiguous situations and difficult decisions are an everyday reality for police officers, whose potential discomfort is soothed by a strong sense of moral legitimacy.

This sense of moral legitimacy depends in part, as Douglas suggests, on erecting boundaries between good and bad, between pure and polluted.[5] The first two sections of this chapter focus on the central social boundary the police construct — between themselves and the "bad guys." The first section focuses on the processes by which the police vilify citizens who, in their eyes, are motivated by evil intentions to plague an otherwise peaceable citizenry. In the second section I discuss how, by contrast, the police view themselves as ardent defenders of the "good people" and their rights to the safe enjoyment of life and property. The third section works from this distinction to discuss how ideas of morality shape not only how the officers view themselves and others but also how they understand the purposes of their actions. In this sense, such territorial actions as jailing are seen not just as mere invocations of the law but as means to protect the good people from fear and harm. I conclude the chapter by reflecting on the overall importance of a moralistic frame for the internal meaning-making practices of police officers and discuss some of the paradoxes inherent in police morality.

The issue of morality has arisen in previous discussions of the police. Banton and Bittner, for example, describe public morality as exercising greater power over police actions than the law does, and thus see it as an important element in structuring police discretion.[6] In this sense, the relevant morality is external to the police; it is something to which the police react. Manning also discusses the role of a larger moral order in the life of police departments. His argument focuses on the moral image the police convey to the public in order to attain legitimacy, their attempt to portray "a sense of sacredness or awesome power that lies at the root of political order" as a means of winning public support and compliance.[7] As useful as these insights may be for understanding police-public relations, they do not sufficiently capture how morality helps officers derive an *internal* sense of justification and co-herence, how it helps them understand and value the various actions they undertake. It is not just that officers react to moral understandings or merely adopt moralistic poses to win public support, but that they develop a fundamental, inter-nally defined purpose for their interventions in people's lives. A central component in the construction of police morality is the identification of undesirable others.

Constructing Evil

Police define themselves in opposition to "others" whom they perceive as dangerous or as potential rivals in adventurous chases. The police starkly define those "others" as evil and dirty, vile and verminesque. The term "bad guy" is ubiquitous in police parlance, augmented at times with such terms as "knucklehead," "asshole," "idiot," "terrorist," and "punk." A "bad guy" is not only an opponent who gives officers a chance to demonstrate their prowess and competence, but also an inferior being against whom they can define themselves as moral agents. The police are thereby defending against not just law-breaking, but against evil itself.

> A sergeant is giving roll-call training. The day's topic is traffic stops of passenger vans. The focus is on safely detaining vans, and particular attention is paid to their numerous doors and windows. Each of these portals, it is suggested, represents a po-tential avenue for a gun attack against the detaining officer. The sergeant emphasizes the maintenance of good lines of sight and careful practices as an officer approches a van. In discussing the possibility of hostile action, the sergeant repeatedly mentions the "vermin" who plague the streets of Los Angeles, the people who do not "have a life." Passengers in vans may be people who are "choosing evil," people who may be capable of indoc-trinating even young children into attacking police officers.

The emphasis in this training is on safety, but the normative order of morality is invoked as well in the way the sergeant encourages officers to view a potential van stop. The people in the van, he reminds them, might attack the police, in large part because they are evil—so evil that they could turn children against the police. The officers may confront not simply danger, but the opponents of goodness.

In this case, the police represent the good, but the citizens whom the "bad guys" plague are also viewed by the police as "good people" whose interests deserve protecting. From this perspective, daily life in Los Angeles is composed of encounters between the evil and the good in which the former damage the latter. Especially bad guys are sometimes referred to as "predators," a term that invokes the sense in which evil attacks good; like carnivores attacking their prey, bad guys pose a clear threat to the peaceable enjoyment of life and property.

Protecting the Vulnerable

Bad guys are a special threat, in the view of police officers, to those who are most vulnerable, namely, children and the elderly. A senior lead officer, for example, expresses frustration at drug dealing in a neighborhood adjacent to an elementary school because she "wouldn't want [her] children to see that." A sergeant in vice expresses the same concern about dice games in a fast food restaurant's parking lot; it is not a sight, he says, that passing motorists would want their children to witness. Several officers try to patrol public parks as often as possible to ensure that children can play there without fear or risk. And another senior lead regularly pressures a group of youths who, she suspects, are dealing drugs in front of an elderly woman's house. The woman has called the senior lead and explained that she is so scared of the men that she will not leave her house. Enraged and protective, the senior lead tells the youths that unless they leave the area, "Somehow, some way, you are going to jail." In each of these cases, officers express a strong desire to protect the weak and vulnerable, those who are most susceptible to the polluting threats of "bad guys."

> *The call concerns a domestic dispute. The officers enter the apartment to discover that a woman has left her husband and infant. They also discover broken plates, evidence of the argument that preceded her flight. The husband proclaims his lack of responsibility for her actions, saying that she was irrational. What most upsets him is the fact that he is left alone with the baby, whose care he seems unprepared to assume. The officers listen with some patience to his protests about her behavior, but reply consistently with a single concern—that the baby's welfare be guaranteed. "The most important thing here," one officer repeatedly states, "is that this baby be taken care of." Eventually, they secure a promise from the man that he will call his best friend's wife to care for the baby. As they leave, the officers express disgust with the man's inability to provide basic care for his child.*

> *A call comes over the radio regarding a family dispute that involves children who have been threatened by a parent. The call is broadcast widely, the sergeant explains, because the police expect to be called back to the location at some later time. The call provides some basic background information that will be useful to them, he says. In particular, any officers who respond will know that children may be in imminent danger. For this reason, the sergeant affirms that the broadcast is a good idea.*

The concern for children extends beyond patrol officers. A dispatcher, for instance, anxiously follows developments in a case involving a runaway juvenile; she monitors each radioed dispatch with obvious concern. When the youth is eventually returned to her home, the dispatcher cheers loudly.

Dirt and Cleansing

As Douglas suggests, those who are evil and dangerous are frequently associated with uncleanliness.

> *A senior lead on patrol points out a hamburger stand that is of interest to him because young men he considers gang members loiter there and because the owner is reputedly involved in dealing drugs. The officer suspects that drugs are distributed at the stand by the owner to the gang member customers. The place, he says, is "dirty, filthy dirty."*

Morally impure areas are often viewed as places where violence is a norm, even a "fact of nature." As a result, police use of violence in these areas is seen by some as unavoidable. This moralistic frame of reference undoubtedly makes it easier for some officers to condone their use of force in minority-dominated areas, which are those most likely to be constructed as impure.

Bad people and places are considered dirty, and police responses, violent and otherwise, are understood in terms of cleansing. Thus, senior lead officers inform each other of the need to "clean up" areas where bad guys prey upon citizens. Such areas are described as "cancers," which can spread unless they are met with the cleansing agent of forceful and persistent police attention. Again, because minority areas are the ones most regularly defined as impure, they are most likely to be deemed candidates for aggressive actions aimed at eradicating the malignancies of alleged evil. Further, the heavy-handedness of some police moralizing makes it difficult for some officers to avoid castigating an entire area, and all its inhabitants, as troublesome. Indiscriminate and needlessly violent policing can be an unfortunate consequence of strict adherence to an overly ardent morality.

This concern with cleansing helps explain the repugnance police feel for graffiti. The various "tags" across the division are potent symbols of the moral disorder that evil gang members spread through a neighborhood and must, the police reason, be swiftly removed to resanitize the area. To clean the graffiti is to clean the area of the too-obvious stain of evil.

Implicit in this notion of cleansing is an image of the police as the opposite of the evil vermin who eat away at community happiness. Indeed, the act of defining the bad guy as other is simultaneously an act of self-definition; as opponents of the bad, the police are thereby defined as virtuous protectors of the good.

Constructing Virtue

If the vermin are infesting the otherwise good neighborhoods of Los Angeles, it follows that the police are the virtuous agency of eradication, the specially trained and courageous force able to confront and overcome evil. In such an embrace of virtue, the officers construct themselves as more than just enforcers of law, more even than courageous, strong, safe, and competent. In a more profound and overarching way, the normative order of morality provides a potent self-definition for the police. They are the agency of last recourse, allocated the responsibility of responding when no one else can or will. They are equipped and coordinated, able to confront people and situations that others shun. They face the predators and haul them off to jail, allowing the "good people" to live in peace again. Confronting and defeating bad guys not only demonstrates prowess and competence, but also is an exercise of virtue and right.

The police sense of virtue combines courage and sacrifice in the course of protecting good from evil. In the language of William Parker, the police are the "thin blue line" separating social order and chaos. This image is preserved in the LAPD as the title of the officers' union newspaper. Parker's sense of the police as a moral force was strong and explicit:

> There are wicked men with evil hearts who sustain themselves by preying upon society. There are men who lack control over their strong passions, and thus we have vicious assaults, many times amounting to the destruction of the life of a fellow man. To control and repress these evil forces, police forces have existed, in some form or another, throughout recorded history.[8]

This moralistic fervor was upheld by Parker's protégé, Daryl Gates, who served as chief from 1979 to 1993:

> Society flinches from the truth: we do our very best to find psychological and sociological reasons to excuse behavior that our minds won't accept for what it is. You walk into court and you have all these attorneys explaining away all of the things that you can sum up in one simple word: Evil.[9]

Police officers are, in other words, engaged in an ages-old battle between good and evil.

The Ultimate Sacrifice

An inescapable aspect of joining the battle between good and evil is that officers risk making the "ultimate sacrifice" in defense of citizens' right to enjoy their lives and their property in peace.

A veteran officer is responsible for a "scenario" at a division training day. In the scenario, two officers stage a domestic dispute. In two-person teams, other officers respond to the situation as they deem tactically appropriate. The veteran officer explains the scenario at the outset and reviews the officers' actions after each session. In the playacting, the officers, a man and a woman, scream loudly at each other in Spanish. As the squabble proceeds, the man pulls a gun and threatens the woman with it. The responding officers face a crucial decision forced upon them by the scenario: should they shoot the man? Shooting the man poses certain risks, primarily should the officers not shoot well. If the man is not disabled by the shot, he may shoot either the woman or the officers. If the officers do nothing, however, the woman's life remains in danger.

At the end of the day, the veteran officer discusses the other officers' responses. He suggests that the officers differed along generational lines. Older officers were more prone to shoot, younger ones to exercise caution. He explains this difference with reference to the fallout from the Rodney King incident and the younger officers' increased fear of facing organizational sanctions should they misuse force. He sympathizes with their concern and acknowledges the clear threat that the situation poses to the life and career of the officers. On the other hand, he says, "I'm the police." It is his final statement on the matter.

By saying "I'm the police," the officer summarily announces that his task is to protect the lives of others even if he has to risk his own. His role as a police officer, he believes, is to protect the woman regardless of the potential cost to himself; it is his ultimate virtue as a police officer that he will embrace that risk. Taking risks is preserved as a department value in part through Medals of Valor, given annually to officers who put their own lives in danger to assist others. It is also preserved via the pictures of four officers—the four Wilshire officers who have died on duty—that hang in the lobby of the division's station.

A sergeant responds to a call: a burglar alarm is ringing at a residence. He parks his car just down the street from the house

but leaves the engine running. He explains to me that he is do-
ing this so that if he should get into trouble, I can escape easily
and quickly. He does not expect me to endanger myself in an
attempted rescue; indeed, he clearly states that I should escape
to safety.

This scenario further illustrates how officers often define themselves: their jobs implicitly contain the possibility of fatal sacrifices for those they are sworn to protect.

For the moral officer, police work is, in the words of one sergeant, "not a job but a vocation," not a set of bureaucratically defined duties but a higher calling. In this sense, officers make a distinction between "going by the book" and "doing the right thing." It may, for example, be bureaucratically safe not to shoot in the domestic dispute scenario described here, but it would not, according to this line of thought, be the right thing to do, because the normative order of morality defines values beyond career comfort or advancement. In this case, it encourages officers to embrace an opportunity to demonstrate virtue by intervening in a situation others might shun. This sense of duty explains, for many officers, why efforts to marshal a work stoppage during contract negotiations met with only haphazard results; too many of them were unwilling to leave the city unprotected. It also explains why officers worked long and arduous hours after the Northridge earthquake without significant complaint. Given a clear call to serve the city, the officers responded virtuously.

Manipulating Morality

The penchant for officers to construct themselves in moral terms can be manipulated by both supervisors and suspects.

At roll call a lieutenant is observing that his officers seem to
be ignoring calls toward the end of the watch. He explains that

he does not know if this is occurring because all of the officers
are tied up with other calls or because they are avoiding working
overtime. This is less important to him than the fact that the calls
"must be answered." Answering the calls, he says, "is the right
thing to do."

At another roll call, the training session focuses on ethics. The
assistant watch commander, a sergeant, reads a scenario that in-
volves an unnecessary use of force by a sergeant, witnessed by
a patrol officer. What should the patrol officer do? A protracted
discussion of various options available to the officer ultimately
focuses on which ranking officer the officer should contact to
report the sergeant's conduct.[10] *At the end of the discussion,*
the watch commander, a lieutenant, asks, "What is the big issue
here?" "Liability," a patrol officer immediately says. There is
laughter in response, but the officer appears to be sincere. The
lieutenant says no, the big issue is that what the sergeant did
"simply isn't right. It is the wrong thing to do."

In both of these scenarios, the supervisors attempt to use
the normative order of morality to motivate the officers into
certain courses of action. Aware of the importance of morality in structuring police behavior, the lieutenants attempt to
mobilize it to ensure officer compliance with department man-
dates. This strategy is available not only to supervisors but
also to suspects.

A vice officer is discussing her regular routine of patrolling
Washington Boulevard, home to many prostitutes. She complains
that the longer she works the street, the more the prostitutes at-
tempt to manipulate her. They often attempt to get familiar with
her, greeting her amicably and inquiring about her health and
welfare. If she decides to arrest them, they play on her conscience.
"Why do you want to do this?" they ask. "You know I have
kids I have to support." The vice officer is obviously uncom-
fortable as she relates this story; she is aware of the difficulty of

*the womens' lives, and she does indeed feel guilty for causing
them short-term harm.*

To this point, I have tried to explain how the normative
order of morality shapes how police officers conceptualize
themselves and others. This occurs in large part through the
construction of the complementary discourses of good and
evil, which helps the police define themselves as morally upright while defining their opponents as morally repugnant and
the spaces those opponents occupy as polluted. The discussion
has also begun to anticipate the ways in which morality provides
a framework that helps the police to define their daily practices.

Morality in Territorial Action

*A sergeant responds to a call regarding a domestic dispute. He
and a patrol team arrive at the same time, and the three officers
knock on the door. The male member of the household answers
the door and allows the officers inside. They discover the man's
wife with a bruise on her face and observe that the telephone has
been pulled from its jack. The officers wonder aloud who called
the police, why the woman has a bruise, and why the phone is
off the wall. Both parties mumble noncommittal responses. The
sergeant and one of the patrol officers take the woman into another room, where she admits that she called the police.*

*The officers explain to her that her husband, by law, must go
to jail; any clear evidence of abuse, in this case the woman's fresh
bruise, requires that the assailant be arrested. She objects. The
sergeant explains that the law requires a jailing. And besides, he
says, her husband's abuse "simply isn't right." The sergeant explains that with the husband out of the house, she will have a
short measure of peace in her life and will be able to get at least
one good night's sleep. The man is taken to jail.*

In this situation, the officers' course of territorial action is
dictated by a law that gives them no significant leeway. When

the woman objects, the sergeant supplements his legal authority with a moral argument: the woman is unnecessarily a victim of actions that "simply are not right." The sergeant attempts to convey to the woman that the officers are providing her a valuable service by freeing her, at least temporarily, from someone who has harmed her. In this instance, the police are not just enforcing the law; they are acting in accord with a moral order that condemns interpersonal violence.

The Morality of Jailing

In this situation, the acts of entering private space and arresting the man are understood not strictly as legal imperatives but also as moral actions with clear benefits for an otherwise tormented woman. The police thereby invest their territorial actions with deep moral significance, transforming them from mere legal acts into ethically correct ones; they protect vulnerable and battered women, not just a legal order. They take the man from his home to jail because it is legal *and* right, and in so doing they construct their actions in terms of a moral normative order.

Police officers frequently construct jailings in these terms. Although capturing a suspect is an aspect of enforcing the law and is often an outgrowth of an officer acting to appear courageous and competent, it is also regularly seen as a means by which officers restore peace to a troubled community. At a community meeting announcing the establishment of a task force to focus on the neighborhood surrounding Smiley and Hauser, the officer in charge loudly proclaims to the crowd, "We want to put bad guys in jail so that you can raise your families in peace." This statement could be construed as public posturing, but it illustrates how the act of jailing is often defined as a good and right act, a means by which officers can bestow peace on tormented and powerless neighborhoods.

Jailing is the most satisfying way in which the police can cleanse a dirty area; it is a surgical dislodging of the cancerous agents that pollute the lives of the good people.[11] It is, in this sense, a satisfying moral act, a clear victory of good over evil, an active removal of the problem and a restoration of peace and tranquility. Jailing erects moral boundaries between good and bad people: the bad are physically separated from the good; they are literally locked up so their cancerous effects are eliminated. Space is thereby purified of its moral pollution,[12] and a sense of order is ostensibly restored. This moral significance of jailing helps to explain further police frustration at what officers perceive to be a lax judicial system that too easily allows the bad back into the community and thus limits police capacity to enact clear moral and physical boundaries between good and evil. In other words, the police capacity to act as a moral agent is compromised, in their eyes, by a judicial system that weakens their most potent and unambiguous means of cleansing a neighborhood.

Moral Suasion

The normative order of morality invests active police intervention in people's lives with a deep sense of significance. It also motivates officers' conversations with those they encounter, particularly those who are acting in ways the officers find troublesome. They focus particularly on young men who appear to be involved with gangs. In these situations, the officers try to do more than just enforce the law; they attempt to steer people from the bad to the good, to supplement their formal coercive powers with exhortations toward right action. Thus, officers talk to young men about the color of their clothes, often a badge declaring affiliation with a gang, and encourage them to move on to a new wardrobe and a more responsible phase of adulthood. They ask young men hanging out on street corners when they are going to move into another way of life that involves the responsibilities of family and job. When a young man told a sergeant that he already had fathered two children, the sergeant only increased the vehemence of his argument, maintaining that hanging out on the street was no way for a responsible father to behave. A similar argument was made by a senior lead officer who attended a meeting at an apartment building where drug dealing was suspected. The SLO admonished the young men who were thought to be dealing for imperiling their neighbors' safety and quality of life.

In these situations, the officers believed that by interfering in people's lives they could be not just agents of the law but also agents of positive change. They tried to show people the errors of their ways and the advantages of taking another course. They explained that certain actions simply "are not right," that they conflict with broader, more valuable courses of action that imply responsibility and good citizenship. They lectured suspects about how the neighborhood is troubled by their actions, how they scare people by taking over street corners and engaging in illicit criminal activity. They countered arguments that young minority people have limited options by invoking the necessity of strong positive action in the face of obstacles.

In this way, the officers acknowledged the limited capacity of the law to influence people's behavior. Though they often embrace the legally justified act of jailing as a means of transforming a community's moral order, they often encounter people, particularly young people, in situations in which no laws have been broken. Encounters on street corners, for example, may not represent an enforcement of the law as much as an assertion of police authority in the name of the good. Officers who believe that it is not right that citizens cannot walk the streets at Smiley and Hauser without fear may feel compelled to patrol the area regularly. They undoubtedly will encounter young people in public space there and will confront them with the fears of the "good people" in mind. In such confrontations, officers are likely to invoke the advisability of another course of action, a reorientation toward the more conventional paths of jobs and adult responsibilities. In this situation, while they are aware that the group may be engaged in illegal activities, the officers are more concerned with asserting their power to restore peace to the neighborhood; they use whatever powers of moral suasion they possess to invoke allegiance to alternative ways of life. They push the youths toward conventionality as a means of upholding a larger moral order that they seek to preserve and defend.

Recognition of a larger morality may indeed, as Banton and Bittner suggest, lead an officer to ignore a strict enforcement of the letter of the law. This is particularly obvious in the case of street vendors, a class of "criminals" most officers are reluctant to jail. The vast number of these vendors are indeed violating the law yet merit little attention from the officers, because the vendors exhibit the very characteristics the officers invoke in dealing with, say, the gang members at Smiley and Hauser: the vendors possess diligence and initiative in a bare-bones struggle for mere survival; they face tremendous odds yet persevere doggedly. Most officers respect these traits and thus prefer to turn a blind eye to illegal vendors; they typically act against vendors only when citizens complain. Again, the officers act according to a broader set of considerations than just the law; the normative order of morality enables the officers to view themselves and their actions as in keeping with a broader set of values that celebrates the good.

Purposes and Paradoxes of Police Morality

The overarching moral order that police officers construct, it should be clear, influences the way they construct and seek to control the spaces they patrol. It thus provides a way to define their territorial actions and to imbue those actions with meaning. This pervasive morality provides not only meaning for daily actions, but also a refuge from the ambiguity and contentiousness that inheres in most police actions. The distinct boundaries between good and evil simplify and justify police actions that might otherwise be open to question. They help obscure the fact that the police usually act against someone's interest and do so in situations that are rarely coherent. In domestic disputes, for example, the wellsprings of the situation are usually impossible to untangle. But this is only the most obvious example of the inchoate social situations in which the police intervene. Behind each scenario the police confront is a history that, if it were investigated, undoubtedly would complicate any decision to intervene. The police, however, not only must make such decisions, but often must do so quickly and forcefully.[13] Ambiguities thus cloud the imperative to resolve situations as efficiently as possible so that order can be restored and the officers can move on to other calls. Always present in the back of every officer's mind is the fact that intervention may require recourse to a force that can maim or kill. The prospect of such violence itself poses difficult moral dilemmas, which are made all the more complicated by the fact that force is typically exercised in quickly evolving situations in which the officers must react with little forethought.

In the face of inherently ambiguous situations that may require sudden recourse to deadly force, it is perhaps understandable why the normative order of morality is so regularly invoked by police officers. The more clear-cut categories of good and evil help resolve the tensions that ambiguity creates and help justify actions, deadly or otherwise, that clearly run against the interests of at least some citizens. The potential ill effects of police intervention are assuaged by investing police action with a sense of moral rightness. By situating their actions within an overarching, transsituational order, the officers not only cleanse neighborhoods of evil but also cleanse themselves of the troubling prospect that their actions can and will harm others.

The paradoxes of this moralistic stance should be obvious. In defining areas as dirty, the officers simultaneously threaten to condone actions that contradict their image as protectors. This is most historically evident in the minority-dominated areas that have complained ardently about police excesses. If the officers easily define people or areas as dirty, they can just as easily forgive aggressive acts aimed at cleansing and thereby undercut the very moral ground upon which they wish to stand. Even in less dramatic and less racially charged contexts, tension between doing good and doing harm is always present. A strong sense of morality may provide a temporary respite from the discomfort of this tension, but morality also feeds the tension by holding the police to standards that their daily practice, which inescapably is coercive, ultimately cannot satisfy.[14]

Conclusion

It should now be clear that the police regularly construct themselves and their actions in accordance with the normative order of morality, which provides a broad set of ethical justifications for many of their practices. It assists them in defining their opponents and themselves via the clear frames of bad and good, and it invests their actions with a sense of moral rightness. Jailing a suspect thereby becomes more than just an enactment of a legal mandate; it is an eradication of poisonous vermin from a needlessly plagued neighborhood. Police intervention in the lives of citizens represents more than just an opportunity to uphold the law, win peer respect, or demonstrate strength; it is an opportunity to be an agent of the good, to defend peace and freedom. From this perspective, police territoriality enables citizens to enjoy their lives and raise their children free from the polluting effects of the bad guys. By removing the evil from the good and segregating it in jail, or by invoking their powers of moral suasion to entice youths along another path, the police attempt to create a better world in accordance with the normative order of morality. Such a moral order obviously imbues police action with a deep sense of meaning by providing an ethical system in which officers locate themselves and their daily interventions in civil society. Actions become more meaningful if they are understood in terms of moral rightness and goodness, in terms of the overarching goals of peace and freedom. Officers are thus doing more than just enacting the law; they are providing an environment in which children can be raised safely, where frail old women can enjoy life without fear.

I have now examined each of the six normative orders that structure police territoriality. In conclusion, I review my argument, consider the relations between the six orders, and survey the various lessons my analysis provides.

9. MAKING AND MARKING SPACE WITH THE LAPD

WHETHER THEY ARE ACTING TO enforce the law, to obey a bureaucratic dictate, to demonstrate masculine prowess, to ensure safety, to display competence, or to enact morality, police officers regularly secure territory as a means of exercising social control. Territoriality is clearly a central component of police behavior, and it is structured by the six normative orders of law, bureaucratic control, adventure/ machismo, safety, competence, and morality. These orders are constellations of rules and practices that, because they are centered on a celebrated value, provide structure and meaning to police actions. In constructing and controlling space, police officers enact some or all of these normative orders.

This last chapter seeks to draw the work together. In the first section, I briefly restate my argument, reviewing the centrality of territoriality to everyday police practice and making the case for the analytic value of the concept of normative order to explain the impulses behind that territoriality. The second section focuses on the relations between the various orders. Here, the value of normative order is again obvious because it helps capture the variegated, complicated, and conflictual reality of police subculture; since the normative orders do not always cohere, internal political strife is an everyday reality in the police world. The third section draws instructive lessons for the study of the three areas of principal concern here — territoriality, the state, and the police. In this final section I therefore attempt to elucidate as precisely as possible the value of my work as well as survey its limits.

Making and Marking Space: A Review

My two principal arguments can be succinctly summarized: territorial action is a fundamental component of everyday police behavior, and such action is structured by six normative orders that provide sets of rules and practices centered on primary values.

The myriad examples of police action discussed in the previous chapters illustrate the former argument. Whether they are enforcing the legally defined boundary between private and public space, clearing areas of people and activities that threaten common notions of public order, constructing a perimeter to capture a fleeing suspect, or removing a spouse abuser to jail, the police regularly control people and seek to create social order by controlling space. In fact, without any effective power over movements through space, police officers would possess very little power indeed. Territoriality, in other words, is a fundamental component of police power, and it is exercised in many police encounters with citizens. It can be exercised dramatically when, say, the police storm a house to capture a barricaded suspect, or more casually when officers separate a feuding mother and daughter to help establish calm. Police attempts to establish order, to establish, in Giddens's terms, "internal pacification," rest upon effective control of space.

This argument sits comfortably within a neo-Weberian emphasis on the importance of territorial control for effective state power. It also accords with a Foucauldian emphasis on the increasingly fine-grained nature of the tactics of the disciplinary network. Police territorial power, in other words, pumps like blood through the body geopolitic and helps secure compliance with the state's legal and moral order. By coercively enforcing the law that principally constitutes state power, and by using moral suasion to modify unacceptable behavior, police officers, through securing the territory they patrol, help tie the scattered threads of state concern together; the police serve as a fundamental line of support for the state's administrative and disciplinary efforts. Police capacity to exercise authority over space fundamentally undergirds overall state efforts to legally control and supervise its people.

This line of thought, however, should not obscure the limitations of Weberian and Foucauldian frameworks for a comprehensive understanding of police territoriality. Overemphasis on the more formalized and centralized legal and bureaucratic impulses of state action (Weber) or on power as the primary dynamic of the disciplinary network (Foucault) obscures the variety of impulses that structure police territorial practice. The concept of normative order provides a means of incorporating the insights of Weberian and Foucauldian work without losing a necessary comprehensiveness. A normative order is a set of rules and practices that, because it is centered on a primary value, not only structures behavior but also provides it with meaning. By sketching a range of normative orders, and by elucidating their structuring influence on police territoriality, we can incorporate the formal and the informal, the bureaucratically stipulated and the sub-culturally constructed, the social and the cultural. We can also incorporate the cognitive and the normative, the rules that people follow and the meanings they create. We can incorporate structure and action, the normative orders and the territorial practices they spawn. And we can bring together macro and micro, not only by investigating the presence of state power in the everyday actions of police officers, but also by elucidating normative orders of varying scope, from the wide parameters of the law to the more confined rules regarding officer safety. As a result, the concept of normative order provides a means to get beyond traditional oppositions—between cognitive and normative, between objective and subjective, between structure and agency, between society and space, between macro and micro—within social and social-geographical thought.

An approach that mobilizes the concept of normative order has the added advantage of capturing the conflict that exists as a fundamental aspect of social life. In this case, it helps to elucidate the internal political struggles that are a basic component of the police world.

On the Relationships between Normative Orders

Police subculture, like other subcultures, is often treated as a unified whole. Attention is often paid to the division between supervisors and patrol officers, but police departments frequently are treated as coherent units governed by group-wide patterns. While coherence is at times obvious in the police world, especially where bureaucratic control is strong, conflict is also always present. The concept of normative order provides a means for understanding this conflict. Although any given normative order possesses a certain legitimacy and power, it may conflict with another order. If, say, a patrol officer decides to pursue a fleeing felon but is called off the chase by a superior officer, normative orders come into conflict. The patrol officer is interested in demonstrating his adventurousness, his competence, and his morality; he wants to test his courage, to overcome an explicit challenge to his authority, and to rid the area of an evil menace. At the same time, however, he may wish to guarantee his and others' safety and to protect his career against the potential damage from ignoring a command. Both continuing and giving up pursuit are simultaneously supported and challenged by conflicting normative orders.[1]

What is of interest here is not just that the normative orders conflict but also that the patrol officer, in the moment he hears the order to cease the pursuit, faces a decision. Because normative orders do not always cohere, significant room is left for human agency. In this case, the officer must choose between conflicting structures of action, between contrasting constellations of rules and values. Either choice presents the potential rewards and disincentives of different normative orders: should the officer risk bureaucratic censure in hopes of winning respect for his bravery, or should he safeguard his career advancement and risk seeming weak? The conflicting reality of the range of normative orders that structure his practice places the officer in a tenuous political situation and forces difficult choices upon him. The existence of a variety of normative orders in the police subculture, in other words, gives birth to interorganizational conflict as different groups choose one order, or set of orders, against others. This helps to explain, for example, the persistent conflict between management and patrol officers. Management is motivated by concerns of legality, control, and safety, thereby guaranteeing the continued dissatisfaction of the patrol officers, who are more typically motivated by concerns of adventure, competence, and morality.

These normative orders may spawn conflict not only within the organization but also between the police and the community. For example, officers who engage in high-speed pursuits to demonstrate their masculine prowess may endanger uninvolved citizens. If they are strongly wedded to adventure, they may shun developing the interpersonal skills so necessary to a vast number of police calls. Further, they may disparage the openness toward the citizenry trumpeted by community policing efforts, preferring to see themselves as a courageous paramilitary force that expertly controls space rather than as a social service agency dedicated to such comparatively mundane concerns as graffiti.

The Role of Race and the Question of Reform

Police-community tensions are most pronounced, of course, in areas populated largely by minorities. Officers are most likely to define these spaces as unsafe and morally unclean, to most actively seek in them the dangerous "other" against whom they can react with strength and bravery. Thus, though they are rarely expressed overtly, racial considerations do affect how officers choose to enact territoriality and do inflame relations with minority communities. Undue cautiousness leads officers to stop and search anyone they fear may be capable of attack; excessive morality fails to distinguish those who warrant scrutiny from those who pose no threat; and ardent masculinity condones excessively harsh tactics against a potential foe. Minority residents thus understandably complain about the choices officers make in defining areas and devising territorial tactics. In other words, officers need not be overtly racist to reinforce tensions between the police and minority communities; as in much of American society, racial matters are expressed subtly, in this case through the choices officers make in enacting one normative order rather than another.[2]

A patrol force wedded to strong senses of adventure, competence, and morality understands itself as a dynamic set of powerful experts dedicated to exercising their tactics to expunge evil from the streets. It therefore chafes at public concern about its occasional excesses of force, because such concerns undeservedly limit officers' capable exercise of authority. This resistance is particularly strong in the LAPD, whose cultural traditions have long reveled in its reputation as an "ass-kicking" department and thus pronouncedly stress the importance of aggressive, forceful action. Police supervisors, because they are more attuned to public concerns than street-level officers are, also incur wrath when they "cave in to politics" and endorse measures to restrict police force. The struggle between LAPD supervisors who want to redraw a public image contrary to the one posed by the Rodney King beating and patrol officers who want to maintain their sense of power and prestige is thus a conflict between different normative orders that structure police practice. Chief Williams's efforts to reshape the culture of the department away from adventure/machismo have met with mulish recalcitrance among the rank and file, who vilify him regularly in their informal conversations and in their monthly newspaper. The ultimate resolution of this struggle is difficult to predict.

The Lessons of Analyzing Police Territoriality

This analysis is the first to subject the practices of police territoriality to explicit and detailed investigation. Only a few previous ethnographic analyses of the police have discussed territoriality, and none has done so in the comprehensive fashion elaborated here. This is somewhat surprising, given

the centrality of making and marking space for everyday police behavior, and given the recent increase in theoretical attention to the territorial practices of state agencies of social
regulation and control. The actual processes of state territoriality have not heretofore received detailed investigation,
however, and thus many of these theoretical insights have
not been subjected to detailed empirical investigation. The
present analysis therefore fills an important gap in studies
about territoriality, the state, and the police and provides
lessons for the analysis of each.

Territoriality

Sack puts forward a definition of territorial action that rightly
focuses on the control of people and resources via the control of area.[3] This not only rejects the more ethological strains
of territorial analysis but also focuses attention on the maintenance of social order via the control of space. Sack perhaps
overstates the case when he argues that territoriality is "*the*
means by which society and space are interrelated," but he
does draw important attention to how social order is predi-
cated upon territorial action.[4] In many ways, my analysis
supports and deepens this insight by explicating how territorial action undergirds police power and, by extension, state-
induced social control. Territoriality is indeed a common police strategy for coordinating social control by coordinating
spatial movements.

At the same time that my analysis has sought to deepen
this important insight of Sack's, it has also attempted to
move away from his tendency to emphasize the formal and
the abstract. Sack is surely right to emphasize the importance of the conceptual emptiability of space in structuring
modern views of territory and the necessary role of large so-

cial organizations in making these views of space more pervasive. In the case of police territoriality, it is clearly useful to emphasize the importance of such formalized structures as the law and bureaucratic control. Nonetheless, territoriality is also shaped by less formal and less abstract impulses. Officers who roust loiterers from a private space are indeed emptying a space based upon the abstract geometrical lines surrounding the property. However, they are also acting as competent and moral agents by asserting their authority and cleansing the area of what they see as an unwanted infestation. Any discussion of territoriality should therefore be sensitive to the variety of ways in which space can be defined and the variety of impulses that motivate control of space.

Contests over space can, of course, mean many things, and they are inextricably intertwined with contests over power and prestige. For the police, the opponents are typically criminal suspects, but they can also be innocent citizens and even other officers. In most instances, officers seek to locate, contain, and capture those they suspect of criminal wrongdoing. In others, however, they may restrict the movements of people who are not involved when they stop someone for information or erect a perimeter around a residential block. They may also struggle with other officers in their attempt to "own the scene" so that they can determine how the tactical control of the area proceeds. In all of these contests, the officers' values and practices are structured by the variety of normative orders that constitute their social world. My analysis is thus an attempt to capture the full richness of territoriality via an expansive examination of its structuring influences. As an analysis of police territoriality, the work is also an investigation into the microgeopolitics of state power.

The State

This work is an explicit attempt to build on Weberian and Foucauldian insights, which are especially significant because they articulate a relationship between state power and spatial control; they discuss the microgeopolitical foundations of state rule. An examination of the practices and effectiveness of police territoriality provides an opportunity to see precisely how the state secures power by securing territory. It also enables an understanding of how state actors construct themselves in the process of constructing and controlling space.

Again, the number and variety of the normative orders of police territoriality create a large set of structuring influences on the exercise of state power. Formally bound by the law and bureaucratic control, police practices are less formally structured by other normative orders of varying scope and construction. Police officers are not depersonalized automatons resulting from formalized flowcharts; they are actively involved in constructing themselves as adventurous, competent, and moral. Their territorial practice is imbued with a deep sense of right and purpose; indeed, it is constructed most grandly in terms of a virtuous victory of good over evil. Police officers therefore intervene in people's lives not just because the law says that they must, but also because they wish to demonstrate their own personal strength, competence, and virtuousness. Territorial intervention is thus a normative endeavor aimed in part at the moral betterment of the community.

This line of thought resonates with recent work that seeks to elucidate the moral underpinnings of state power (see chapter 8). My fieldwork reveals the moral intent to create a more positive and upright citizenry that is behind much police action. It goes a step further, however, by underscoring how moral considerations provide a strong internal justification of police actions because it helps obscure the complicated reality of the situations police officers face and the troubling consequences of their actions for at least some citizens.

This focus on the variety of normative orders that structure the practices of a state agency such as the police and the ongoing internal struggle among the orders questions the coherence that is often attributed to the state. It is important, therefore, as Abrams suggests, to avoid reifying the state as some sort of coherent, transcendental unity, and instead to focus on state practices and their often contradictory structuring influences.[5] Such a focus delves beneath the legitimating protective cover that an image of coherence can provide the state and reveals the internally fragmented nature of actual state practice.

A comprehensive and probing view of state action must capture both its formal and informal structures; it must capture the variety of motivations underlying attempts to create and enforce state order. Such an analysis provides lessons about the nature of state power generally defined and also, more specifically, about the power of the police.

The Police

It should be obvious by now that the world of the police is a complex one, structured as it is by the various normative orders that implicitly compete for allegiance. As they secure space, officers enact one or many of these normative orders; as they make and mark space, they make themselves law-upholding, bureaucratically controlled, adventurous, safe, competent, and moral agents of police power. Just which order, or combination of orders, will capture a particular officer's allegiance at any given time eludes prediction; the outcome is dependent on varying political shifts and individual agency. The overall strength of one order versus another, however, is a central political struggle within all police departments.

From this perspective, it is possible to gain perspective on current reform efforts in Los Angeles and elsewhere aimed at instituting community policing. This reform movement seeks to destroy the walls the professional model erected between police and community and to engage the two sides in various cooperative endeavors to secure public order. Implicit in this effort is a reduction of the autonomy historically granted the police. The police are increasingly urged not to consider themselves a detached, professionalized, and exquisitely trained force, but a service beholden to the community on terms defined by the community.

This reform movement is spreading within the police profession as a response to a variety of failures of the professionalized model, not the least of which is public disenchantment with a detached and often aggressive police force. It is typically championed by supervisors who, by virtue of their political positions, are more directly affected by pressure from the community. In choosing to implement this reform movement, supervisors mobilize the normative order of bureaucratic control to ensure compliance from the ranks below. The troops resist these bureaucratic impulses because they fear a diminution of their capacity to act as courageous, competent, moral agents. Indeed, community policing, with its emphasis on working closely with the citizenry, is a deliberate move away from the professional model of policing, exemplified by the LAPD, which implied detached experts who solved problems of crime with their specially developed skills.

On the other hand, it is precisely the manner in which these troop-centered normative orders have historically been reproduced that motivates community policing in the first place. Adventurous cops sometimes take risks that endanger citizens; competent cops sometimes take offense at those who flee and dole out a violent "payback" in response; and moralistic cops can draw rigid boundaries between good and evil, such that those who dress or behave in certain ways elicit immediate and excessive suspicion. Community policing can therefore be understood as a concerted effort to blunt the excesses of many of the normative orders of police territoriality.

Still, unless police reformers address an officer's needs to feel strong, safe, competent, and virtuous, reform movements will meet with significant and possibly crippling resistance. This concern in part explains why community policing is usually accompanied by efforts to support "problem-oriented" policing, which is designed to give individual officers more investigative leeway in their patrol areas. This is a potentially fruitful way of assuring individual officers that their territorial actions will carry some measure of normative significance that resonates with their sense of themselves as competent, strong, and virtuous. There remains the possibility, however, that reinforcement of the normative orders of competence and morality will continue to fuel a disdain for community oversight of police practice. In other words, officers may feel a continued desire to be regarded as experts beyond the pale of citizen concern. It is likely that the various normative orders that structure police practice will remain in perpetual conflict and that the political state of any given police department will reflect a particular, and possibly temporary, arrangement of relative power between those orders.

On the Limits of This Analysis

My discussion of community policing introduces the actors who have largely remained silent throughout this analysis, namely, the citizens who are policed. These actors have appeared as objects of police attention, as trophies to capture or good people to protect, as quarries in pursuits, as potential prey. Their voices and their motivations have been obscured. This is an unfortunate slight that robs the analysis of an even fuller discussion of police practices, since little attention is directed toward the *effects* of those practices on citizens. This is unfortunate precisely because community policing is so much in the wind; the analysis provides few insights into how such a reform movement could best be implemented.

Future work, therefore, must listen to and incorporate these voices. As valuable as elucidation of the internal workings of territoriality may be for understanding everyday police practice, it is an incomplete picture. The present work provides a useful place to start by providing a comprehensive picture of how the police define and seek to control space. Alternative conceptions of space and proper spatial order exist within the citizenry, and with them alternative conceptions of how the police can or should define their territorial role. A fuller explication of the politics of police territoriality needs a more explicit and developed engagement with these alternative conceptions, particularly if community policing continues to progress as a reform movement. The present work, it is hoped, provides important insights into one side of the dialectic between police and community. It is the challenge of future work to more fully investigate the other.

Future work might also profitably examine other realms of policing, including aspects of public policing beyond patrol and also the growing role of private police in the surveillance and control of space. Especially in cities like Los Angeles, the private security apparatus is becoming a significant factor in the overall geopolitics of urban space. And beyond physical space lies the world of cyberspace, where policing is also a key question. A full investigation of the relationship between the control of territory and effective policing would have to encompass these realms.

"The Demand for Order in Civil Society," in David Bordua (ed.), *The Police: Six Sociological Essays* (New York: Wiley, 1967).

21. Monkkonen, *Police in Urban America 1860–1920*.

22. Robert Fogelson, *Big-City Police* (Cambridge, Mass.: Harvard University Press, 1977).

23. For a historical account of the difficulty of establishing centralized control over provincial police departments, see Miles Ogborn, "Ordering the City: Surveillance, Public Space and the Reform of Urban Policing in England 1835–56," *Political Geography* 12 (1993): 505–21. For a discussion of how the enforcement of the same law varies across space, see Nicholas K. Blomley, "Law and the Local State: Enforcement in Action," *Transactions, Institute of British Geographers* 13 (1988): 199–210. These analyses highlight the local character of most police agencies and thus implicitly problematize the coherence of the state assumed by much neo-Weberian work; there is a perpetual tension concerning the division of responsibilities between state agencies at different levels. In terms of policing, this division is important. Although federal law enforcement agencies are of increasing significance in the United States, their functions are largely devoted to detective work. As a result, the active work of patrolling, particularly in public space, devolves to local agencies. Local police thus exist as a primary interface between citizens and the state. See William A. Geller and Norval Morris, "Relations between Federal and Local Police," in Michael Tonry and Norval Morris (eds.), *Modern Policing* (Chicago: University of Chicago Press, 1992), 231–348.

24. Jeffrey C. Alexander, *Theoretical Logic in Sociology,* vol. 3, *The Classical Attempt at Theoretical Synthesis: Max Weber* (Berkeley and Los Angeles: University of California Press, 1984).

25. Roger Friedland and Robert R. Alford, "Bringing Society Back In: Symbols, Practices, and Institutional Contradictions," in Walter W. Powell and Paul J. DiMaggio (eds.), *The New Institutionalism in Organizational Analysis* (Chicago: University of Chicago Press, 1991), 232–63; Bob Jessop, "Capitalism, Nation-States and Surveillance," in David Held and John Thompson (eds.), *Social Theory of Modern Societies: Anthony Giddens and His Critics* (Cambridge: Cambridge University Press, 1989), 103–28.

26. Some representative samples include Michael Brown, *Working the Street: Police Discretion and the Dilemmas of Reform* (New York: Russell Sage Foundation, 1981); Richard Ericson, "Police Bureaucracy and Decision-Making: The Function of Discretion in Maintaining the Police System," in Jack Goldsmith and Susan Goldsmith (eds.), *The Police Community* (Pacific Palisades, Calif.: Palisades Publishers, 1974), 84–97; and Maurice Punch, *Conduct Unbecoming: The Social Construction of Police Deviance and Control* (London: Tavistock, 1985).

27. Michel Foucault, *Discipline and Punish: The Birth of the Prison* (New York: Vintage, 1977), and *Power/Knowledge* (New York: Pantheon, 1980).

28. For a more theoretical discussion, see John Lowman, "Conceptual Issues in the Geography of Crime: Toward a Geography of Social Control," *Annals, Association of American Geographers* 76 (1986): 81–94. For more empirically focused pieces, see Matthew Hannah, "Space and Social Control in the Administration of the Oglala Lakota ('Sioux'), 1871–1879," *Journal of Historical Geography* 19 (1993): 412–32; and Jennifer Robinson, "A Perfect System of Control? State Power

and 'Native Locations' in South Africa," *Environment and Planning D: Society and Space* 8 (1990): 135–62.

29. David Garland, *Punishment and Modern Society: A Study in Social Theory* (Chicago: University of Chicago Press, 1990), ch. 7; and Felix Driver, "Bodies in Space: Foucault's Account of Disciplinary Power," in C. Jones and R. Porter (eds.), *Reassessing Foucault: Power, Medicine and the Body* (London and New York: Routledge, 1994), 19–34.

30. Felix Driver, "Power, Space and the Body: A Critical Assessment of Foucault's *Discipline and Punish*," *Environment and Planning D: Society and Space* 3 (1985): 425–46; Alan Hunt, *Explorations in Law and Society: Toward a Constitutive Theory of Law* (London and New York: Routledge, 1993); Bob Jessop, *State Theory: Putting Capitalist States in Their Place* (University Park: Pennsylvania State University Press, 1990); and Nicos Poulantzas, *State, Power and Socialism* (London: New Left Books, 1978).

31. See Steve Herbert, "The Geopolitics of the Police: Foucault, Disciplinary Power, and the Tactics of the Los Angeles Police Department," *Political Geography* 16 (1996): 47–57.

32. Mark Granovetter, "Economic Action and Social Structure: The Problem of Embeddedness," *American Journal of Sociology* 91 (1985): 481–510; William Sewell, "A Theory of Structure: Duality, Agency and Transformation," *American Journal of Sociology* 98 (1992): 1–29.

33. Sherry Ortner, "Theory in Anthropology Since the Sixties," *Comparative Studies in Society and History* 26 (1984): 126–66; Robert Wuthnow, *Meaning and Moral Order: Explorations in Cultural Analysis* (Berkeley and Los Angeles: University of California Press, 1987).

34. For a definition of normative order, see Talcott Parsons, *Structure of Social Action* (New York: McGraw-Hill, 1937), 91–92.

35. See Paul J. DiMaggio and Walter W. Powell, introduction to Powell and DiMaggio (eds.), *New Institutionalism*, 1–38; and John C. Heritage, *Garfinkel and Ethnomethodology* (Cambridge: Polity Press, 1984), chapters 2 and 3.

36. Sewell, "A Theory of Structure."

37. Margaret Archer, *Culture and Agency: The Place of Culture in Social Theory* (Cambridge: Cambridge University Press, 1988); Ulf Hannerz, *Cultural Complexity* (New York: Columbia University Press, 1992).

38. This is the dominant theme of the selections included in Gregory and Urry (eds.), *Social Relations and Spatial Structures*. See also Edward Soja, *Postmodern Geographies: The Reassertion of Space in Critical Social Theory* (London and New York: Verso, 1989).

39. This is an issue raised in various ways in such works as David Bayley and Harold Mendelsohn, *Minorities and the Police* (New York: Free Press, 1968); Egon Bittner, "The Police on Skid-Row: A Study in Peace Keeping," *American Sociological Review* 32 (1967): 699–715; Keith, *Race, Riots and Policing*; and John Van Maanen, "Working the Street: A Developmental View of Police Behavior," in Henry Jacob (ed.), *The Potential for Reform of Criminal Justice* (Beverly Hills: Sage, 1974).

40. J. Nicholas Entrikin, *The Characterization of Place* (Worcester, Mass.: Clark University Press, 1991).

41. My focus is primarily on the social construction of space rather than its material characteristics. It is clear, however, that officers develop ideas about areas in part based upon their physical and demographic characteristics. "Anti-police" areas, for example, are materially disadvantaged and dominated by minority residents. Thus, while my focus is on the ideas about spaces that officers develop and reaffirm, these ideas are developed with material conditions in mind.

42. See, for example, Kay Anderson, "Cultural Hegemony and the Race-Definition Process in Chinatown, Vancouver: 1880–1980," *Environment and Planning D: Society and Space* 6 (1988): 127–49; Peter Jackson, "Street Life: The Politics of Carnival," *Environment and Planning D: Society and Space* 6 (1988): 213–28; and Andrew Merrifield, "The Struggle over Place: Redeveloping American Can in Southeast Baltimore," *Transactions, Institute of British Geographers* 18 (1993): 102–21.

43. John Agnew, *Place & Politics* (Winchester, Mass.: Allen & Unwin, 1987); James Duncan, *The City as Text: The Politics of Landscape Interpretation in the Kandyan Kingdom* (Cambridge: Cambridge University Press, 1990); and Doreen Massey, "The Political Place of Locality Studies," *Environment and Planning A* 23 (1991): 267–81.

2. The Setting and the Research

1. The outside patrol units will actually be assigned by the dispatchers who work downtown in the Communications Division and have primary responsibility for assigning calls to officers. The helicopters and dogs can be requested by officers but will not respond to all, or even most, requests.

2. I was also extremely fortunate to attend the grievance session that was part of the training days. At that session, the officers were encouraged to express their frustrations openly, and they did so readily.

3. I asked Michael Hooper, who recently retired from the LAPD after twenty-three years of service, to read the manuscript for verification. Now a professor of criminal justice, Hooper, in a personal letter, said that I "captured the essence of policing in Los Angeles."

3. The Law and Police Territoriality

1. This point is made repeatedly in a variety of works that deal with a variety of police forces. See Michael Banton, *The Policeman in the Community* (London: Tavistock, 1964); David Bayley and Harold Mendelsohn, *Minorities and the Police* (New York: Free Press, 1968); Egon Bittner, "The Police on Skid Row: A Study in Peace Keeping," *American Sociological Review* 32 (1967): 699–715, and "Police Discretion in the Apprehension of Mentally Ill Persons," *Social Problems* 14 (1967): 278–92; Herman Goldstein, "Police Discretion: The Ideal vs. the Real," *Public Administration Review* 23 (1963): 140–48; Wayne LaFave, *Arrest: The Decision to Take a Suspect into Custody* (Boston: Little, Brown, 1965); and Jerome Skolnick, *Justice without Trial* (New York: Wiley, 1966).

2. For a useful review of this literature, see Laurie Brooks, "Police Discretionary Behavior: A Study of Style," in Roger Dunham and Gerry Alpert (eds.), *Critical Issues in Policing* (Prospect Heights, Ill.: Waveland, 1989), 121–45. See also Donald Black, *The Manners and Customs of the Police* (New York: Academic Press, 1980); Michael Brown, *Working the Street: Police Discretion and the Dilemmas of Reform* (New York: Russell Sage Foundation, 1981); Richard Lundman, Richard Sykes, and John Clark, "Police Control of Juveniles: A Replication," in Richard Lundman (ed.), *Police Behavior: A Sociological Perspective* (Oxford: Oxford University Press, 1980), 130–51; William Muir, *Police: Streetcorner Politicians* (Chicago: University of Chicago Press, 1977); Harvey Sacks, "Notes on Police Assessment of Moral Character," in David Sudnow (ed.), *Studies in Social Interaction* (New York: Free Press, 1972), 280–93; and Richard Sykes and John Clark, "Deference Exchange in Police-Civilian Encounters," in Lundman (ed.), *Police Behavior*, 91–105.

3. Bayley and Mendelsohn, *Minorities and the Police*; Jonathan Rubinstein, *City Police* (New York: Farrar, Straus and Giroux, 1973); Carl Werthman and Irving Piliavin, "Gang Members and the Police," in David Bordua (ed.), *The Police: Six Sociological Essays* (New York: Wiley, 1967).

4. Bittner, "Police on Skid Row."

5. Banton, *Policeman in the Community*.

6. Bittner, "Police Discretion in the Apprehension of Mentally Ill Persons"; Richard Ericson, *Making Crime: A Study of Detective Work* (Toronto: University of Toronto Press, 1981); Peter Manning, *Police Work* (Cambridge, Mass.: MIT Press, 1977).

7. The best introduction to this work is Nicholas K. Blomley, *Law, Space and the Geographies of Power* (New York: Guilford, 1994). See also Nicholas K. Blomley and Gordon C. Clark, "Law, Theory and Geography," *Urban Geography* 11 (1990): 433–46; Gordon C. Clark, "The Geography of Law," in Nigel Thrift and Richard Peet (eds.), *New Models in Geography* (London: Unwin Hyman, 1989), 310–33; David Delaney, "Geographies of Judgement: The Doctrine of Changed Conditions and the Geopolitics of Race," *Annals, Association of American Geographers* 83 (1993): 48–65; Steve Herbert, "The Trials of Laurence Powell: Law, Space and a 'Big Time Use of Force,'" *Environment and Planning D: Society and Space* 13 (1995): 185–99; and Westley Pue, "Wrestling with Law: (Geographical) Specificity vs. (Legal) Abstraction," *Urban Geography* 11 (1990): 566–85.

8. Representative examples include Alan Hunt, "A Theory of Critical Legal Studies," *Oxford Journal of Legal Studies* 6 (1986): 1–39; Allan Hutchinson, *Dwelling on the Threshold: Critical Essays on Modern Legal Thought* (Toronto: Carswell, 1988); Mark Kelman, *A Guide to Critical Legal Studies* (Cambridge, Mass.: Harvard University Press, 1987); and Roberto Unger, *The Critical Legal Studies Movement* (Cambridge, Mass.: Harvard University Press, 1986).

9. Mark Blacksell, Charles Watkins, and Kim Economides, "Human Geography and Law: A Case of Separate Development in Social Science," *Progress in Human Geography* 10 (1986): 371–96; Jack Kress, "The Spatial Ecology of Criminal Law," in Daniel Georges-Abeyie and Keith Harries (eds.), *Crime: A Spatial Perspective* (New York: Columbia University Press, 1980), 58–71.

10. Roger Grimshaw and Tony Jefferson, *Interpreting Policework* (London: Allen Unwin, 1987).

11. Max Weber, *Max Weber on Law in Economy and Society* (New York: Simon and Schuster, 1954), 5.

12. Manning, *Police Work*.

13. Police officers are especially upset with offenders who run from them, which not only offends them as a challenge to their authority but also constitutes, for them, prima facie evidence of a crime (see chapter 7).

14. Values other than law enforcement also shape how officers rate their interest in working different beats. These other values are discussed in subsequent chapters.

15. Felony arrests are included in the monthly "recaps" (accounts of their activities) compiled for each officer. It is commonly accepted in the LAPD that a high number of felony arrests demonstrates competence.

16. The charge of prostitution requires evidence of an actual solicitation, which patrol officers are extremely unlikely to overhear. For this reason, prostitution is almost exclusively dealt with by vice officers, who deploy special undercover units.

17. In practice, officers do not necessarily end up spending all, or even most, of their shift in their Basic Car Area. As a result, while they all have their preferences for which area to work, many of them do not believe that their assignment is especially relevant in determining where they actually patrol on a given shift.

18. Nicholas Fyfe, "Space, Time and Policing: Towards a Contextual Understanding of Police Work," *Environment and Planning D: Society and Space* 10 (1992): 469–81; Arthur Stinchcombe, "Institutions of Privacy in the Determination of Police Administrative Practice," *American Journal of Sociology* 64 (1963): 150–60.

19. A few months later, I observed the gang unit spend about two hours in surveillance of the house, hoping to detect activity that would justify arrests. This more detached strategy was their response to the grandmother's refusal to allow an easy transgression of the public-private boundary.

20. The fieldwork ended before I had an opportunity to discern the effectiveness of the raids.

21. Robert David Sack, *Human Territoriality: Its Theory and History* (Cambridge: Cambridge University Press, 1986), 20.

22. Another way of developing an appreciation for the importance of the boundary is to consider the spatial reaches and permissible actions of public versus private police officers. In general, private police have easy access to spaces that stand outside the reach of public police and often can pursue a wider range of control tactics. See Clifford Shearing and Philip Stenning, "Modern Private Security: Its Growth and Implications," in Michael Tonry and Norval Morris (eds.), *Crime and Justice: An Annual Review of Research* (Chicago: University of Chicago Press, 1981), 193–245; and Nigel South, "Reconstructing Policing: Differentiation and Contradiction in Post-War Private and Public Policing," in Roger Matthews (ed.), *Privatizing Criminal Justice* (London: Sage, 1989), 76–104.

23. See Rubinstein, *City Police*; Werthman and Piliavin, "Gang Members and the Police."

24. The audacity of some officers in intimidating citizens is most compellingly illustrated in William Chambliss, "Policing the Ghetto Underclass: The Politics of Law and Law Enforcement," *Social Problems* 41 (1994): 177–94. See also Richard Ericson, *Making Crime: A Study of Police Detective Work* (Toronto: University of

Toronto Press, 1981); and Diane McBarnet, "Arrest: The Legal Context of Policing," in Simon Holdaway (ed.), *The British Police* (London: Edward Arnold, 1979),
24–40.

25. See Herbert, "The Trials of Laurence Powell."

26. Officers tell each other that unless they are careful, they will be "rooming
with Stacey," a reference to Sergeant Stacey Koon, one of the two officers involved
in the King beating who served prison sentences.

27. Officers often will not arrest people with outstanding warrants, especially
in the case of gang members. An outstanding warrant provides leverage over individuals who may have knowledge of a crime the police are investigating. If an individual is arrested and serves sufficient jail time to clear the warrant, that leverage
evaporates.

4. The Bureaucratic Ordering of Police Territoriality

1. Robert Fogelson, *Big-City Police* (Cambridge, Mass.: Harvard University
Press, 1977).

2. Samuel Walker, *A Critical History of Police Reform* (Lexington, Ky.: Lexington Books, 1977).

3. James Gazell, "William H. Parker, Police Professionalization and the Public: An Assessment," *Journal of Police Science and Administration* 4 (1976): 28–
37; Joseph Woods, "The Progressives and the Police," Ph.D. dissertation, University of California, Los Angeles, 1973.

4. Woods, "Progressives and the Police."

5. Martin Schiesl, "Behind the Badge: The Police and Social Discontent in Los
Angeles since 1950," in Martin Schiesl and Norman Klein (eds.), *20th Century Los
Angeles: Power, Promotion and Social Conflict* (Claremont, Calif.: Regina, 1990),
153–94.

6. Orlando Wilson, *Parker on Police* (Springfield, Ill.: Charles Thomas, 1957).

7. California Advisory Committee to the United States Commission on Civil
Rights, *Police-Minority Relations in Los Angeles and San Francisco* (Washington,
D.C.: United States Commission on Civil Rights, 1963); Robert Fogelson, "White
on Black: A Critique of the McCone Commission Report," in Anthony Platt (ed.),
The Politics of Riot Commissions, 1917–1970 (New York: Macmillan, 1971), 307–
34; William Turner, *The Police Establishment* (New York: Putnam, 1968).

8. Michael Brown, *Working the Street: Police Discretion and the Dilemmas
of Reform* (New York: Russell Sage Foundation, 1981); Richard Ericson, "Police
Bureaucracy and Decision-Making: The Function of Discretion in Maintaining the
Police System," in Jack Goldsmith and Susan Goldsmith (eds.), *The Police Commu-
nity* (Pacific Palisades, Calif.: Palisades Publishers, 1974), 84–97; Peter K. Manning,
The Narcs' Game (Cambridge, Mass.: MIT Press, 1980); Maurice Punch, *Conduct
Unbecoming: The Social Construction of Police Deviance and Control* (London:
Tavistock, 1985); Elizabeth Reuss-Ianni, *Two Cultures of Policing* (New Brunswick,
N.J.: Transaction, 1984); Jerome Skolnick, *Justice without Trial* (New York: Wi-

ley, 1966). Of these researchers, only Brown studied the LAPD. The similarity of the analyses, however, suggests a fairly common pattern in police agencies.

9. Egon Bittner, "The Police on Skid Row: A Study in Peace Keeping," *American Sociological Review* 32 (1967): 699–715."

10. Manning, *Narcs' Game,* 96.

11. Punch, *Conduct Unbecoming*; Reuss-Ianni, *Two Cultures of Policing.*

12. This is a common argument among the "new institutionalist" work on organizations. For general statements, see Paul DiMaggio and Walter Powell, "Institutional Isomorphism and Collective Rationality," *American Sociological Review* 48 (1983): 147–60; and John Meyer and Brian Rowan, "Institutionalized Organizations: Formal Structure as Myth and Ceremony," *American Journal of Sociology* 83 (1977): 340–63. For examples of new institutional analyses of policing, see John Crank, "Watchman and Community: Myth and Institutionalization in Policing," *Law and Society Review* 28 (1994): 325–51; and John Crank and Robert Langworthy, "An Institutional Perspective of Policing," *Journal of Criminal Law and Criminology* 83 (1992): 338–63.

13. Jonathan Rubinstein, *City Police* (New York: Farrar, Straus and Giroux, 1973).

14. Concerns of adventure/machismo, safety, competence, and morality are intimately bound up in decisions over whether and how to intervene, as succeeding chapters will illustrate.

15. Such an act constitutes a felony offense, which explains the off-duty officer's interest.

16. As it turns out, this was not the first time this officer had acted to strongly assert his authority; his rashness had by this point earned him enmity of more than one sergeant.

17. The highest ranking of a patrol officer is "P-3," also known as a field training officer. In other words, a P-3 is senior enough to serve as a training officer for probationary officers fresh out of the academy. An especially aggressive sergeant is derisively referred to as a "P-4," to indicate an apparent desire to remain a patrol officer instead of becoming a more-detached supervisor.

18. Reuss-Ianni, *Two Cultures of Policing.*

19. In a survey of LAPD officers assessing how they would respond to hypothetical situations, Brown found that officers interested in promotions were less likely to take aggressive actions. Brown, *Working the Street.*

20. Not all members of the command staff are seen as unsympathetic to the plight of the "troops." One Wilshire lieutenant, for example, was called a hero by one officer because he had been a driving force in getting the department to approve the use of pepper gas as an intermediate level of force. The officers perceived the need for such an option because "upper body control holds" had been designated a potentially lethal use of force in the 1980s after the deaths of several suspects and because the baton had been severely discredited as a use of force after the Rodney King incident.

21. Indeed, the term *politics* attracts significant scorn from many officers. Some of them, without facetiousness, go so far as to describe Stacey Koon and Laurence Powell, the two officers convicted for the King beating, as "political prisoners." One sergeant even compared the two to Gandhi.

5. Adventure/Machismo and the Attempted Conquest of Space

1. The literature on the police subculture is significant. Perhaps the most useful survey is found in Robert Reiner, *The Politics of the Police* (Toronto: University of Toronto Press, 1992). Much of this literature treats police subculture as coherent and monolithic. My analysis differs by emphasizing the conflictual, complex, and contradictory nature of the world the police construct and inhabit. See also Victor Kappeler and Geoffrey Alpert, *Forces of Deviance* (Belmont, Calif.: Waveland, 1994).

2. Many of the officers of the LAPD are women, and some of them exhibit the more typically "masculine" characteristics described here. Others tend to adopt a less confrontational approach to police work. This issue is explored in greater detail later in the chapter.

3. James Richardson, *Urban Police in the United States* (Port Washington, N.Y.: Kennkat, 1974); Samuel Walker, *A Critical History of Police Reform* (Lexington, Ky: Lexington Books, 1977).

4. Ed Cray, *The Enemy in the Streets* (Garden City, N.Y.: Anchor, 1972); James Gazell, "William H. Parker, Police Professionalism and the Public: An Assessment," *Journal of Police Science and Administration* 4 (1976): 28–37; Jerome Skolnick and James Fyfe, *Beyond the Law: Police and the Excessive Use of Force* (New York: Free Press, 1993).

5. Janis Appier, "Juvenile Crime Control: Los Angeles Law Enforcement and the Zoot-Suit Riots," *Criminal Justice History* 11 (1990): 147–70; Edward Escobar, "The Dialectics of Repression: The Los Angeles Police Department and the Chicano Movement," *Journal of American History* 79 (1993): 1483–514.

6. Quoted in William Turner, *The Police Establishment* (New York: Putnam, 1968), 80.

7. Quoted in Robert Cipes, *The Crime War* (New York: New American Library, 1967), 134.

8. Mike Davis, *City of Quartz: Excavating the Future in Los Angeles* (London: Verso, 1990); Robert Fogelson, *The Fragmented Metropolis: Los Angeles, 1850–1930* (Cambridge, Mass: Harvard University Press, 1967).

9. To "buy a call" means to radio your intention to handle it. A "hotshot" is a call that requires an immediate police response because someone's life may be in some danger. By definition, a hotshot represents a potential confrontation with a suspect who may be armed and dangerous.

10. Alarmingly, one officer, holding his shotgun on a stakeout following a shooting at a hamburger stand, said to me, "I can shoot a suspect as easily as I can take a shit."

11. This is vividly illustrated in Sanyika Shakur, *Monster: The Autobiography of an L.A. Gang Member* (New York: Penguin, 1993).

12. Martin Sanchez Jankowski, *Islands in the Street: Gangs and American Urban Society* (Berkeley and Los Angeles: University of California Press, 1991).

13. Code 3 is the highest-priority coding a call can be given by a dispatcher; the responding units are to use lights and siren to arrive as quickly as possible.

14. This tendency to overstate the danger of the situation may have been influenced by the proximity of the roller rink to the station, the ultimate safe haven. The station may have appeared somewhat vulnerable if random shots were echoing nearby.

15. The incompatibility between "social work" and adventurousness is well explicated in Egon Bittner, "Florence Nightingale in Pursuit of Willie Sutton: Toward a Theory of the Police," in Herbert Jacob (ed.), *The Potential for Reform of Criminal Justice* (Beverly Hills: Sage, 1974), 17–44.

16. Independent Commission on the Los Angeles Police Department, *Report* (Los Angeles: City of Los Angeles, 1991).

17. Women commonly run across this form of bias. See Francis Heidensohn, *Women in Control? The Role of Women in Law Enforcement* (Oxford: Clarendon, 1992), ch. 5.

18. For overviews, see Jack Greene and Stephen Mastrofski (eds.), *Community Policing: Rhetoric or Reality?* (New York: Praeger, 1988); and Mark Harrison Moore, "Problem-Solving and Community Policing," in Michael Tonry and Norval Morris (eds.), *Modern Policing* (Chicago: University of Chicago Press, 1992), 99–158.

19. Wesley Skogan, *Disorder and Decline: Crime and the Spiral of Decay in American Neighborhoods* (Berkeley and Los Angeles: University of California Press, 1990).

20. Independent Commission, *Report*; Skolnick and Fyfe, *Beyond the Law.*

21. The Christopher Commission report quotes the LAPD dispatcher who radioed the fire department for an ambulance to pick up the battered Rodney King as saying, "They should know better than to run. They are going to pay a price when they do that." Independent Commission, *Report,* 14.

6. Safety and Police Territoriality

1. In the wake of the convictions of Stacey Koon and Laurence Powell, one officer at roll call questioned whether he continued to endorse this folk wisdom.

2. Communications Division staff who dispatch the calls say that officers regularly express frustration that they were not informed that a suspect was armed, but those who call 911 are often distraught or are themselves unaware of the dangerousness of the situation; thus the operator's capacity to gather full information is limited.

Tension between dispatchers and patrol officers is a regular occurrence that stems in large part from safety concerns. Officers are dependent on dispatchers not only for specific information about suspects, but also for a basic assessment of the level of seriousness of the case. This assessment is reflected in a dispatcher's decision regarding how to "code" the call. The coding of the call is a measure of how high a priority the dispatcher assigns an immediate officer response; calls that involve an immediate threat to someone's welfare are given high priority. Such calls, of course, carry a greater likelihood that officers will also be endangered. For a thorough analysis of officer-dispatcher communication practices, see Peter Manning, *Symbolic Communication: Signifying Calls and the Police Response* (Cambridge, Mass.: MIT Press, 1988).

3. The habit of walking flush against the front of buildings is so ingrained in some officers that that is how they approach buildings on calls where no danger is evident.

4. Officers also wish to avoid situations in which their vision is blocked or impaired. For example, a sergeant was critical of himself for driving into a setting sun through a narrow alley while he was looking for a dangerous suspect; his temporary blindness made him vulnerable, he said.

5. The police use the term to disguise from a suspect the fact that his or her name has matched the name of someone with an outstanding felony warrant. This enables the police to handcuff the suspect before he or she is aware of what the police know.

6. The young man called the police after killing his father. Then he went outside and waited for the officers. After killing the officer, who was in her first week on the job, the young man went back inside and killed himself.

7. The thought here is that officers may not be able to radio their location in a help call. Indeed, the console on the radio apparatus includes a help button for situations when there is not enough time to use the radio's mouthpiece. If the help button is used, all the dispatcher can do is inform other units of the last known location of the unit. For this reason, dispatchers urge patrol officers to update their location regularly. This poses a problem, however, for officers who wish to hide their location from dispatchers as a means of avoiding additional assignments. For example, patrol officers may not immediately radio in that they have cleared the scene of their latest call because they want to relax or to run an errand. If they encounter unexpected trouble and push their help button, responding units will be directed to the location of the call they just cleared, which may not be the same as their current location.

8. This particular area is commonly referred to as the "mini-jungle," a clear indication that the officers believe that rules of civil conduct do not pertain there. It is called "mini" because it is viewed as a smaller version of an area known simply as the "jungle" in the contiguous Southwest Division of the LAPD.

9. In fact, the sergeant retold the story of my being unprotected many times around the station, and I thereby seemed to gain some measure of respect for being unafraid in that location.

10. When calls are made to 911, information about the phone number appears on the dispatcher's screen. This information includes the address of the phone and whether it is a residence, business, or pay phone.

11. Independent Commission on the Los Angeles Police Department, *Report* (Los Angeles: City of Los Angeles, 1991).

12. Similarly, a map posted at the Air Support headquarters indicates the locations of each of the division stations. A handful are marked as places where violence has occurred, and thus as places where helicopters should regularly fly over. An admonition on the map reads, "If we don't protect them, who else will?"

7. Competence in Police Territoriality

1. Either the officer feared for my safety or he did not want me to witness any use of force, which, the officer might fear, could lead to either or both of the officers getting into trouble.

2. See Nigel Fielding, "Police Socialization and Police Competence," *British Journal of Sociology* 35 (1983): 568–90. Fielding argues that competence varies by task, rank, and audience.

3. Jerome Skolnick and James Fyfe, *Beyond the Law: Police and the Excessive Use of Force* (New York: Free Press, 1993).

4. Veteran officers were especially frustrated at what they perceived to be a tepid response to the shooting. In previous years, they suggested, the department would have been very aggressive in patrolling the area and arresting people for any possible offenses. An aggressive approach would have placed sufficient pressure on the neighborhood so that someone would "give up" the identity of the shooters. The lack of such a response was further proof to these officers of how the department had weakened in the face of public criticism.

5. Jonathan Rubinstein, *City Police* (New York: Farrar, Straus and Giroux, 1973), 166.

6. In one instance, a senior lead officer simply told a street vendor about whom residents were complaining, "Go to where I can't see you."

7. This explains the department's desire to maintain Basic Car "integrity" (see chapter 2). If patrol officers are to be part of close police-community relations, and are to be able to do more autonomous "problem-oriented" policing, they need, according to this logic, to patrol a given area regularly.

8. A worker in the Communications Division developed this point in discussing officer complaints that dispatchers do not provide them enough information regarding the potential dangerousness of suspects. His argument is not only that such information cannot always be obtained from a caller, but also that the officers need to rely on their own eyes and tactics.

9. Van Maanen, "Working the Street."

10. Similarly, Wilshire officers who respond to calls in other divisions are often commended by supervisors for keeping up with their internal call load, being willing to act in the interest of the department as a whole, and countering Wilshire's reputation as a division that requires more help than it provides.

11. William Webster and Hubert Williams, *The City in Crisis* (Los Angeles: City of Los Angeles, 1992), 15.

8. The Morality of Police Territoriality

1. See, for example, Philip Corrigan and Derek Sayer, *The Great Arch: English State Formation as Cultural Revolution* (Oxford: Basil Blackwell, 1985); Jacques Donzelot, *The Policing of Families* (New York: Pantheon, 1979); and Andrew Polsky, *The Rise of the Therapeutic State* (Princeton, N.J.: Princeton University Press, 1991).

2. The classic sociological discussion of this process is Durkheim's discussion of the simultaneous construction of normality and pathology. Emile Durkheim, *The Rules of Sociological Method* (Chicago: University of Chicago Press, 1938), ch. 3. For a general discussion of boundary maintenance and a historical illustration, see Kai Erikson, *Wayward Puritans: A Study in the Sociology of Deviance* (New York: Wiley, 1966).

3. See David Campbell, *Writing Security* (Minneapolis: University of Minnesota Press, 1992); and Simon Dalby, *Creating the Second Cold War: The Discourse of Politics* (London: Pinter, 1990).

4. Corrigan and Sayer, *The Great Arch,* 4.

5. Mary Douglas, *Purity and Danger* (Andover, Mass.: Routledge and Kegan Paul, 1966), and *Natural Symbols* (London: Barrie and Jenkins, 1973).

6. Michael Banton, *The Policeman in the Community* (London: Tavistock, 1964); Egon Bittner, "The Police on Skid Row: A Study in Peace Keeping," *American Sociological Review* 32 (1967): 699–715.

7. Peter Manning, *Police Work* (Cambridge, Mass.: MIT Press, 1977), 4.

8. Quoted in Orlando Wilson, *Parker on Police* (Springfield, Ill.: Charles Thomas, 1957), 5.

9. Daryl Gates, *Chief: My Life in the LAPD* (New York: Bantam, 1992), 165.

10. In the post–Rodney King era, no patrol officer willing to ignore the sergeant's conduct would admit it in roll call.

11. One officer enjoys jailing, he says, because it "gets bad sperm off the street."

12. See David Sibley, "Survey 13: Purification of Space," *Environment and Planning D: Society and Space* 6 (1988): 409–21.

13. As Bittner puts it, "The mission of the police is limited to imposing provisional solutions to uncontexted emergencies." Egon Bittner, *Aspects of Police Work* (Boston: Northeastern University Press, 1990), 11.

14. For an extended treatment of the paradoxes inherent in police use of coercive power, see William Muir, *Police: Streetcorner Politicians* (Chicago: University of Chicago Press, 1977).

9. Making and Marking Space with the LAPD

1. This situation actually occurred in another division of the LAPD during my fieldwork. The patrol officer decided to continue the pursuit, for which he received a long suspension. The suspension was the subject of much ire in the officers' union newspaper. The officers complained that their colleague demonstrated courage and captured a felon, and thus did not deserve such a harsh punishment. In this fashion, the logic of one set of normative orders is used to minimize the legitimacy of another.

2. For a discussion of the subtle expressions of racial considerations in the criminal justice system, see Kathleen Daly, "Criminal Law and Justice System Practices as Racist, White and Racialized," *Washington and Lee Law Review* 51 (1994): 431–64. For more general discussions of the subtle and often coded expression of racial attitudes in the United States, see Michael Omi and Howard Winant, *Racial Formation in the United States: From the 1960s to the 1990s* (New York and London: Routledge, 1994); and David T. Wellman, *Portraits of White Racism* (Cambridge: Cambridge University Press, 1993).

3. Robert David Sack, *Human Territoriality: Its Theory and History* (Cambridge: Cambridge University Press, 1986). See also Edward Soja, *The Political Organization of Space* (Washington, D.C.: Association of American Geographers, 1971).

4. Sack, *Human Territoriality,* 5.

5. Philip Abrams, "Notes on the Difficulty of Studying the State," *Journal of Historical Sociology* 1 (1988): 58–89. See also Claude Denis, "The Genesis of American Capitalism: An Historical Inquiry into State Theory," *Journal of Historical Sociology* 2 (1989): 328–56; and Richard Marsden, "The State: A Comment on Abrams, Denis and Sayer," *Journal of Historical Sociology* 5 (1992): 357–77.

INDEX

Steve Herbert is assistant professor of criminal justice and adjunct assistant professor of geography at Indiana University, Bloomington. He earned a Ph.D. in geography in 1995 from UCLA, where he was also a lecturer. He has also taught at the University of Michigan. He has published articles in *Urban Geography, Environment and Planning D: Society and Space, Political Geography, Annals of the Association of American Geographers,* and *Professional Geographer.*